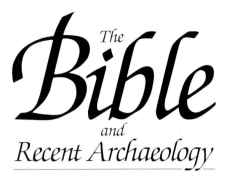

The
Bible
and
Recent Archaeology

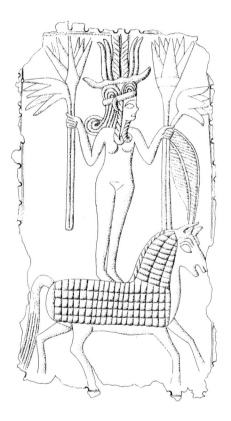

The *Bible*

and

Recent Archaeology

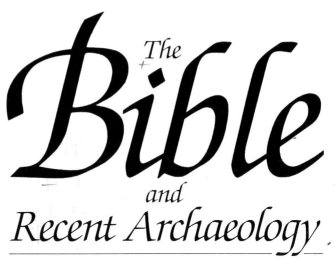

Kathleen M. Kenyon
Revised edition by P.R.S. Moorey

John Knox Press
ATLANTA

Biblical references are taken from the *Jerusalem Bible*. The chronologies of individual rulers are those of J. Bright, *A History of Israel* (3rd edition; 1981).

Library of Congress Cataloging in Publication Data
Kenyon, Kathleen Mary, Dame.
  The Bible and recent archaeology

  Bibliography: p.
  Includes index.
  1. Bible—Antiquities—Addresses, essays, lectures.
I. Title.
BS621.K4 1987   220.9′5   87-45548
ISBN 0–8042–0011–4

First edition © 1978 Kathleen Kenyon
Revised edition © 1987 The Trustees of the British Museum
10 9 8 7 6 5 4 3 2 1
Published simultaneously by British Museum Publications Ltd in
Great Britain
and by John Knox Press in the United States of America, 1987
Printed in Great Britain
John Knox Press
Atlanta, Georgia 30365

Contents

Acknowledgements

Dr Roger Moorey is most grateful to Dr Graham Davies and to Mr Timothy Potts for their valuable comments on the typescript; he alone is responsible for what has survived. He is also indebted to Mrs Jean Dodds for typing up his original manuscript and to Miss Jenny Chattington of British Museum Publications for her editorial advice.

He wishes to thank most warmly the following scholars and their associated expeditions for their assistance in obtaining photographs and for permission to reproduce them here: Prof. N. Avigad (98, 109–11); Mrs C.-M. Bennett (87, 92); Prof. A. Biran (13, 83); Dr K. G. O'Connell, S.J. (96); Dr G. I. Davies (38, 39); Prof. W. G. Dever (59, 63); Prof. Trude Dothan (31, 32, 36); Dr Adnan Hadidi (97); Dr A. Kempinski (43–4); Prof. M. Kochavi and Dr P. Beck (23, 24a, b, 25); Dr A. Mazar (33–5, 45–6); Dr Z. Meshel (76–8); Dr E. Netzer (114–15); Prof. E. Oren (30, 85–6); Mr T. F. Potts (22, 56); Prof. Y. Shiloh (52, 67a); Prof. L. Stager (26–7); Prof. E. Stern (93–4); Mr J. N. Tubb (37); and Prof. D. Ussishkin (41–2, 71–3, 84, 91).

The author and publishers would also like to thank the following institutions for permission to reproduce their photographs: 54–5, 69, 88, 99, 116: the Visitors of the Ashmolean Museum, Oxford; 90: the Trustees of the British Museum; 118: Bureau Technique Commun pour les travaux du restauration du Saint Sepulchre; 53, 64 and 65: the Oriental Institute, Chicago University; 5, 101: Pictorial Archive, Jerusalem (photo Dr Cleave); 6, 103 Rockefeller Museum, Jerusalem. 7, 12, 28, 34, 48, 66, 67b, 70, 89 and 119 were drawn by Karen Hughes. 74, 107 and 108 are the copyright of Dr Moorey; the front cover illustration is reproduced by permission of Mr J. N. Tubb. All other illustrations are the copyright of Mr J. J. Kenyon Todd Ritchie.

Preface to the New Edition

In 1976 the late Dame Kathleen Kenyon (1906–78) delivered the Haskell Lectures at Oberlin College in Ohio, USA. Two years later, in the year of her death, they formed the basis for the first edition of this book under a title chosen intentionally to echo her father's *The Bible and Archaeology*, published in 1940. In many ways it was a strange choice since, in her own words, 'the approach here is very different'.

The training and experience of father and daughter were sharply contrasted. F. G. Kenyon had been educated at Oxford as a classical scholar, was an expert in the textual criticism of the Greek New Testament, and spent his working life in the British Museum, where he was Director when Dame Kathleen began her career. She had been trained at Oxford as a modern historian, was an expert above all in field archaeology, and spent much of her working life in London and Oxford as a university teacher and administrator. In her father's book the progress of Biblical scholarship and the modern reconstruction of ancient Near Eastern history were the primary themes, whilst in hers the evidence of texts is little used and all the emphasis is thrown on the mute evidence of excavations in Palestine.

Both were at one, however, in writing for the general public, not for specialists. In a very special sense Dame Kathleen's lectures (for in the original they read as a spoken rather than as a written text) were a summing up for the interested amateur of her own manifold contributions to Palestinian archaeology. They were the popular complement to her more academic *Archaeology in the Holy Land* (1960), which passed through three editions in her lifetime, and was widely translated. Together they showed how, for over forty years, she had stood at the centre of Palestinian archaeology.

After graduating at Oxford, Dame Kathleen spent the early 1930s excavating, in the summers, with Mortimer Wheeler (1890–1976) at the Romano–British site of Verulamium (St Albans) in England and, in the springs, with the Crowfoots at Samaria in Palestine (1, 2). To Wheeler she was indebted for a rigorous training in the best field techniques of the day; to Crowfoot for her first opportunity to apply a careful method of

Above 1 The hill of Samaria viewed from the south-east, with the village of Sebastiyah on the right. A photograph taken by the Crowfoot Expedition during its excavations at this site between 1931 and 1935. It gave Kathleen Kenyon her first experience of excavating a Near Eastern tell.

Below 2 An exceptionally fine piece of ashlar masonry in the inner wall at Samaria attributed to the first period of building at Samaria in the reign of Omri (*c.* 876–869 BC).

3 Vertical aerial view of the mound (Tell es-Sultan) at Jericho, showing trenches cut by Kathleen Kenyon's expedition (1952–8). At centre right is the long, deep Trench 1, which provided a sequence of superimposed levels of occupation debris from about 8000 BC through to the Byzantine period, though it showed clearly how virtually all occupation after about 1600 BC had been eroded off the top of the mound.

stratigraphical analysis to the debris of a singularly complex Near Eastern mound. From this challenging apprenticeship she evolved what is now widely known as the 'Wheeler–Kenyon' method. Put simply, this requires that the successive layers of debris in a mound should be peeled off in accord with their natural bed-lines (stratigraphy), thus ensuring the accurate isolation of structural phases and related objects, and recorded *on the spot* by careful drawing, photography and written descriptions. This precise method was first fully applied in Dame Kathleen's world-famous excavations at Jericho (1952–8). Her remarkable success in unravelling thousands of years of human settlement, back to remote prehistory, on a site renowned in the Bible, brought her skills and techniques to the notice of all archaeologists. Modified by criticism and wide application in the last thirty years, her methods have become fundamental to the best excavations in the area today. It is her greatest and most enduring legacy.

Inevitably, her many contributions to knowledge, through these excavations and subsequent ones at Jerusalem (1961–7), are gradually being

9

4 The eastern slope of the eastern ridge of the 'City of David' (Ophel) in Jerusalem with the Kidron Valley to the left; the photographer has his back to the Temple platform. In the centre, running down the slope, is the long Trench A cut by the Kenyon Expedition (1961–7) to locate the defences on this side of the Jebusite city and its successors. The Virgin's Well or Spring of Gihon is just beyond the lower end of the trench. The main line of defences revealed by this daring excavation is almost in the centre of the photograph.

modified and superseded to some degree by new material and fresh explanations. She would have been the first to accept this. As all her general books show, she readily appreciated new work, critically assessed it and when convinced, for she was formidable in debate, accepted it as part of her latest presentation of the evidence.

In accepting the publishers' invitation to prepare a new edition of this book a decade after publication I have borne in mind Dame Kathleen's own definition of her purpose: 'The history of the great Empires [i.e. of the Near East] is mainly left in the background as not requiring further description and as part of well-accepted history. The recent archaeology and new historical interpretation are based on excavations mainly carried out or at least published since the Second World War, on the publication and translation during that time of texts recovered in excavations ... and on modern approaches in literary criticism of the Old Testament.' Inevitably, I have moved the lower limit forward to about 1958, the end of her own Jericho excavations, so as to cover the most recent generation of work; but in doing so I have, of course, had to retain many comments on earlier work, not least her own, that is now at the heart of our knowledge of Palestinian archaeology.

With passing time, despite the strife-ridden world of the Near East, archaeological activity there continues to increase as both salvage and research archaeology is everywhere forced to cope more and more with urban expansion, with rural developments and with the demands of military planners; with local departments of antiquities seeking to reveal their national heritage, to preserve it and to present it for tourists; with expeditions growing in size and expertise, concentrating on intensive surface surveys and scientific reconnaissances as well as on excavations; and with the marked impact of the natural and social sciences on archaeology that has stimulated fresh questions, defined new lines of inquiry and radically increased the body of data to be processed.

Nor, in this time, has research in Biblical studies as they relate to archaeology stood still. A period of optimism has recently given way to a pervading sense of scepticism in those areas of study where the two disciplines meet. I have followed the spirit of Dame Kathleen's approach by not entering into the debate over the validity of 'Biblical archaeology' that has engaged many scholars, particularly in the United States, in the decade since her death. 'Biblical archaeology' has long been compromised in the eyes of field archaeologists by its association with a fundamentalist approach that seeks to demonstrate, through the evidence provided by archaeology, the historical reliability or 'truth' of the Bible. It is thus perfectly reasonable for archaeologists of a different persuasion to wish to substitute some other, less equivocal term to describe their activities, though most of the present alternatives are no less politically or ideologically controversial.

The view taken here, as I believe in the original text, is simple. Archaeological evidence, as such, *proves* nothing about the Biblical tradition. It only offers a constant stream of fresh information on antiquity from which to reconstruct the societies of the lands of the Bible, before, during and after the times in which the text we have was written down. From this body of data, if that is the preferred approach, the reader may weigh the probabilities in any critical assessment of the Biblical record. As, like Dame Kathleen, I am neither a philologist nor a textual scholar, the emphasis here is primarily on the non-textual information provided by archaeology for the modern understanding of the Biblical world. I have cited, as she did, the most vital discoveries of extra-Biblical texts and, when appropriate, new interpretations of the historical parts of the Old Testament, but only as background information.

The sharpest indicator of the pace of archaeological discovery on the ground and the lively state of explanatory debates, to any reader who chooses to compare the old and the new editions of this book, will be the extent of my changes; they are numerous, far-reaching and often radical. Dame Kathleen believed, as I do, that the general public should be able to read, in terms they may readily understand, reliable up-to-date reviews of archaeological research that reflect current debates as much as current agreements. This she always gave them, even if it wholly superseded her own earlier researches and publications. It is in this spirit that I have proceeded. In archaeology there is no standing-still. Only I know how much better it would have been, if I had had to argue it step by step with her, as once I had to defend my interpretations of part of her excavations at Jerusalem, where I had the privilege of excavating under her direction long ago.

P. R. S. Moorey
Ashmolean Museum, Oxford,
1986

Chronological table

Egypt Roman Empire	AD	Palestine Roman Empire	AD	Mesopotamia Parthian Period
	BC	(Herod the Great)	**BC**	
Hellenistic Period Ptolemies		Hellenistic Period Ptolemies/Seleucids/ Hasmoneans (142–63 BC)		Hellenistic Period Seleucids
◄················	**330**	Achaemenid Persian Empire	**330**	───────────►
	500	Babylonian Captivity	**500**	
Late Period		Iron Age II B–C Divided Monarchy		Neo-Babylonian Period Neo-Assyrian Period Middle Assyrian Period
		Iron Age II A		
Third Intermediate Period	**1000**	United Monarchy	**1000**	Middle Babylonian Period
		Iron Age I		
New Kingdom		Late Bronze Age II		Kassite Period
	1500	Late Bronze Age I	**1500**	
Second Intermediate Period		Middle Bronze Age II B–C		Old Babylonian Period
Middle Kingdom				
		Middle Bronze Age I (II A)		Isin-Larsa Period
First Intermediate Period	**2000**	Intermediate Period Early Bronze IV– Middle Bronze I	**2000**	Ur III Period
				Akkadian Period
Old Kingdom	**2500**	Early Bronze Age III	**2500**	Early Dynastic III
		Early Bronze Age II		Early Dynastic II
				Early Dynastic I
Proto-Dynastic Period	**3000**	Early Bronze Age I	**3000**	Jamdat Nasr (Uruk III) Period

1. The Old Testament and archaeology

One will always have to reconstruct biblical history by starting with the texts, and the texts must be interpreted by the methods of literary criticism, tradition criticism and historical criticism. Archaeology does not confirm the text, which is what it is, it can only confirm the interpretation we give it.

Père de Vaux in *Near Eastern Archaeology in the Twentieth Century: Essays in Honor of Nelson Glueck* (New York 1970), p. 78.

It is easy to forget that little more than a century ago the Old Testament stood virtually alone as a survivor from the literary traditions of the ancient Near East. Nothing was known of its ancestry nor of the world in which it had been written, save for what might be gleaned from its own pages and from scattered references in the surviving works of Greek and Roman writers. Since the last quarter of the nineteenth century archaeological excavations and chance finds in the Near East and in adjacent regions have transformed our understanding of it.

The Old Testament may remain in many ways unique, but it is no longer without ancestors, relatives and contemporaries. What it shares with the cults and cosmologies, the rituals and myths, the poetry and prose recorded in original texts from ancient Egypt and Western Asia, and the ways in which it differs, may now be seen with increasing clarity. Whether it is history, literature or religion that interests the curious reader of the Old Testament today, the impact of over a century's archaeological research on the study of the text itself is fundamental.

The finding of the Dead Sea Scrolls (see chapter 8) is undoubtedly the most spectacular and significant discovery of our time in its impact on the study of the Hebrew Old Testament. Until the discovery of these texts in the Qumran region none of the manuscripts on which standard editions of the Hebrew Bible were based dated before the ninth century AD. The scrolls, in so far as they cover Biblical texts, take this Hebrew text back a thousand years or more, since some are as early as the mid-third century BC. Before the Qumran discoveries scholars had given special attention to ancient translations of the Hebrew text, since they had been the earliest sources.

The most authoritative of these was the Septuagint translation into Greek, traditionally said to have originated in the work of seventy-two scholars invited by Ptolemy II Philadelphus (*c.* 309–246 BC) to make a Greek translation of the Pentateuch for the famous library at Alexandria in Egypt.

Although the Dead Sea Scrolls dominate the subject, a steadily increasing body of inscriptions in various ancient languages recovered by archaeology, dating from the Late Bronze and Iron Ages, now offer invaluable working tools for textual criticism and literary analysis of the Old Testament. Firstly, such texts reveal the ways in which the Hebrew language, its spelling and writing, evolved during the period in which it is known that the canon of the Hebrew scriptures was being assembled. This historical knowledge allows specialists to interpret words that were previously obscure. Secondly, Israelite literature may now be placed in the context of Canaanite literature, notably through the texts from Ras Shamra (see chapter 3). These have provided much first-hand information about Canaanite religion and

5 Aerial view from the west of the complex of buildings at Khirbet Qumran, near the north-western end of the Dead Sea, excavated by Père de Vaux in 1951–8. The long narrow room on the far right was identified as a place of assembly, sometimes used for communal meals. Channels and cisterns illustrate the importance of the storage and distribution of water in the buildings. This structure is now generally identified as an Essene centre, whose library of manuscripts – the Dead Sea Scrolls – was hidden in adjacent caves early in the First Jewish Revolt against Rome (AD 68–74) (see chapter 8).

religious literature. Such texts have also greatly assisted modern understanding of early Hebrew poetry.

As archaeology has done in the sphere of material culture, this aspect of Biblical Studies has shown that Israel was heir to a richly varied literary tradition which she modified and transformed into her own idiom. However, even when this legacy has been recognised, it is not easy to establish how, when and where it operated upon those generations of writers, some creative, some merely copyists, who made the Old Testament we read. The precise nature of the sources they used, whether written documents or oral traditions, is still not readily established. Nor is there any certainty about the origin and date of such material. In modern western society it is easy to forget that oral tradition has a double meaning, since it embraces both the concept that oral tradition preceded the written and the fact that oral records persisted as a constant check upon, and support for, the written word. In both the Arab and the Jewish tradition of today there are many in the Near East who know not only their scriptures but also the greatest commentaries on them by heart. Thus, at all times even the written texts that survive tell only part of a complex story.

Yet there is one element in the case of the West Semitic region that is so special as to deserve emphasis. Whereas in the rest of the ancient Near East literate societies used complex writing systems generally mastered only by a small scribal élite, Canaan and Israel shared perhaps the most dynamic cultural asset ever devised by man. They invented and developed a system of alphabetic writing: that is, the means to write with less than thirty easily memorised signs any language they chose (see chapter 3). It made the ability to read and write much more accessible. By the time the earliest parts of the Old Testament were written down this tool already provided for an unprecedented accumulation and dissemination of information in writing. This has one consequence of great importance for the evolution of the Old Testament. A written text, relatively easily understood by a wide variety of people, is unusually open to discussion, analysis and modification to suit changing ideologies or new circumstances. Editors and compilers, always more numerous than original authors, found a place of influence in the transmission and interpretation of texts that was at once more powerful and more effective than it was in the closed world of scribes in ancient Egypt or Mesopotamia.

If we were to seek, as a preliminary to this survey of the relationship between the Bible and recent archaeology, the one point of some agreement among modern scholars over the primary stages through which the Old Testament passed in reaching its present form, it would have to be in an apparent link between major historical events and crises and the formation of the literature of Israel. The first event, the emergence of Israel, is the

6 Storage jar of the type used to conceal scrolls in the caves round Khirbet Qumran. This example was restored from sherds excavated in the buildings at Qumran, establishing a link between the settlement, which had its own potters, and the Dead Sea Scrolls.

most obscure and controversial, and the one where it may be hoped that early extra-Biblical texts, revealed by archaeology, will eventually come to allow reliable identification of the oldest elements in the surviving text of the Old Testament.

It has long been assumed from internal evidence that the first great phase of literary activity occurred at the time of David and Solomon. At present the archaeological record offers no direct evidence for or against such an assumption. Then again, it has been deduced from the text of the Old Testament that the fall of Samaria in the later eighth century BC, and of Jerusalem in the early sixth, brought with them major reappraisals of older texts. The Exile in particular, it seems, saw a profound reshaping of earlier texts in the interests of fresh ideological inspiration designed to meet an unprecedented crisis of confidence.

Ironically, in view of many of his later attitudes, it was Albright who, at the beginning of his academic career, in 1918, put his finger on the point all archaeologists and historians need to remember in approaching any part of the Old Testament as an historical source: 'the long memory possessed by semicivilized peoples for historical fact is a pious fiction of over-zealous apologists . . .' This note of caution has now become the guiding light in an increasingly sceptical appraisal of the historical authenticity of many Biblical narratives. As we have noted, two major stages of editorial work at least have probably filtered these texts, one under the Monarchy, when the people of Israel were first seeking to explain their origins and recording them in writing, and another under the Exile and afterwards, when a fundamental crisis needed explanation. On each occasion archaic sources were modified by preconceptions that may well have distorted, even if they did not destroy, their primary historical value.

It is for this reason that the new edition of this book takes a more cautious view at the outset than was the case in the first edition. In doing so, it does not deny the possible existence of archaic fragments interwoven into the text of the Pentateuch as it survives. Indeed, the account of the religion of the Patriarchs, so different from that of later Israel, may be a case in point. But it does take the position that the evidence of textless archaeology, and the very few directly relevant extra-Biblical texts revealed by excavation in the last hundred years, do not yet offer sufficient hard information to isolate with confidence those parts of the text that are sufficiently reliable historically to permit valid reconstructions of the early (or 'proto') history of the Hebrews in Canaan and adjacent lands.

The information provided by excavations proves nothing about the Biblical tradition. Its contribution is quite different. It offers fresh matter, of ever increasing variety and precision, in the weighing of probabilities. It is, obviously, most directly relevant when compared with descriptions of material culture in the Old Testament, as notably the description of Solomon's Temple furnishings. In a wider sphere it elucidates the social, economic and ecological setting in which political events took place. Only the occasional historical inscription, as for example the Mesha Stela from Dhiban or the inscription from Hezekiah's tunnel in Jerusalem help with reconstructing events. Archaeological information relates to time measured in generations rather than in brief periods of years; with the submerged majorities in social systems rather than with their great men or, at best, with the ruling group as a whole rather than as recognisable personalities.

It is with such considerations in mind that this book now begins not with a 'Patriarchal period', as still seemed appropriate to Kathleen Kenyon in 1978, but with Canaan in its Near Eastern setting in the second millennium BC, during the periods known archaeologically as the Middle and Late Bronze Ages. Canaan is the region and the society into which the early historians of Israel believed, when they first came to reflect upon the matter, the fathers of their nation had penetrated as an alien group. It is with the theatre of Israel's earliest history that we may best begin rather than with the leading players, since they, as will become readily apparent, remain invisible to the eye of the archaeologist.

2. When to begin
The problem of the Patriarchs

Just over a century ago, in 1878, rather more than a decade before serious archaeological investigation in Palestine began with Petrie's excavations at Tell el-Hesi, the great German Biblical scholar Wellhausen (1844–1918) had argued that:

Certainly we gain no historical knowledge of the patriarchs, but only of the time when the stories about them emerged in the Israelite period; this later age is here unconsciously projected, in its inner and outer features, back into distant antiquity, and is reflected there like a glorified image . . .

Half a century later, in 1938, after the first major phase of archaeological research in Palestine and neighbouring countries, the American archaeologist and Biblical scholar Albright (1891–1971) epitomised in the following comment the immense optimism bred among some scholars by advances in the new discipline:

Archaeological and inscriptional data have established the historicity of innumerable passages and statements of the Old Testament.

In his estimation, and subsequently in that of his students and many colleagues in the English-speaking world, the Patriarchal narratives in *Genesis* were high on the list of such passages. German scholars of the Old Testament, particularly, were less certain of the value of this archaeological 'proof'.

However, Albright's view was to dominate approaches to the relationship between the Bible and archaeology for a generation. It was widely assumed that the historical value of *Genesis* had been substantially demonstrated with the assistance of archaeological evidence and that its text might consequently serve as a sound basis for all future studies. Then, just over a decade ago, a marked reaction set in, pioneered by two young American Biblical scholars, T. L. Thompson and J. Van Seters. Although they differed in a number of significant ways, they were united in the belief that Wellhausen had come closer to the heart of the matter than Albright had. Albright's methods of inquiry and argument by analogy were forcefully challenged and boldly refuted in the spirit of Thompson's fundamental dictum, published in 1974: 'Archaeological materials should not be dated or evaluated on the basis of written texts *which are independent of these materials*; so also written documents should not be interpreted on the basis of *archaeological hypotheses*' (my italics). This cautious, sceptical view has proved to be very much in tune with the times, though fiercely contested at the outset in some quarters. It has steadily gained ground in recent years, bringing with it a much more pessimistic assessment of the potential role of archaeological information in establishing the value of the earlier parts of the Old Testament as historical sources.

In the following account it is accepted that the Patriarchal stories do not portray a 'Patriarchal period' that may be fixed in time. But it is likely that they do preserve authentic details from the second millennium BC, transmitted, perhaps orally, through the period of Israelite settlement (*c.* 1200–1000 BC), because they played a necessary role in the political and ideological needs of that time. The earliest surviving evidence for any people is a blend of myth and legend from which shreds of historical reality can only be separated, if at all, by rigorous methods of analysis from a much larger body of comparative evidence than is at present available.

During the last fifty years, in books seeking to relate the Bible to archaeology, the 'Patriarchal period' has most often been dated either to some part of the Middle Bronze Age (*c.* 2000–1550 BC), at a time remarkably close to the traditional absolute chronology of Bishop Ussher (AD 1581–1656), for centuries printed in the Authorized Version of the Bible, or to an advanced date in the Late Bronze Age (*c.* 1550–1150 BC), much closer to the emergence of Israel in Canaan (see chapter 5).

In writing of the peoples of the ancient Near East scholars generally adopt Old Testament usage, as when Abraham is described as an 'Aramaean', implying ethnic and cultural distinctions as they would normally be understood. It is, however, important for the layman to understand that often when Near Eastern archaeologists write of 'Akkadians' or 'Hurrians' or 'Amorites', this is more specifically short-hand for 'Akkadian-speaking peoples' or 'Hurrian-speaking peoples' and so on. Ancient peoples are thus identified by their linguistic grouping, either from surviving texts written wholly in their own language or from their distinctive personal names in texts written in other languages. In working thus with personal names it is assumed that a person's name reflects his or her mother-tongue; not invariably the case, of course, but true enough to provide gross information. As many personal names in the ancient Near East were phrases, often invoking a deity's name, as in 'God *x* is my Lord' or 'Servant of Goddess *y*', they offer the student of languages two clues to a person's origin. First, there is the nationality of the deity referred to, and then the linguistic

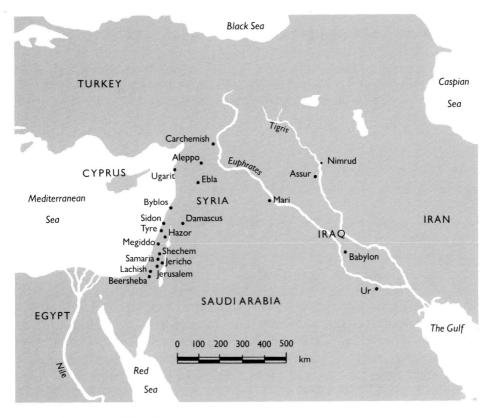

7 Map of the ancient Near East.

identity of the rest of the phrase, revealing the language spoken by the bearer of the name. Such categories often remain arguable.

In the earlier dating of the 'Patriarchal period', favoured in the first edition of this book, the Patriarchs were associated with an interruption in town life at the end of the Palestinian Early Bronze Age (*c.* 2350–2000 BC), marked by destruction levels at this time on a number of sites excavated in Palestine before and immediately after the Second World War. Archaeological evidence was interpreted as indicating a recession in which intrusive nomadic peoples, with a way-of-life taken to be identical with that attributed to the Patriarchs, settled throughout Palestine. Texts from Egypt of the early second millennium BC, ritually cursing the Pharaoh's enemies ('Execration Texts') seemed to endorse this view, whilst nearly contemporary texts from Mesopotamia showed the city-states of Babylonia struggling on their western frontiers with semi-nomadic intruders, known locally as 'Amorites'. It was these Amorites who were thought to have penetrated Palestine from the eastern desert periphery at the end of the Early Bronze Age, causing a hiatus in the development of urban societies. Into this hypothetical Amorite migration Abraham and his followers were ingeniously fitted.

Spectacularly in the middle and later 1970s, with the discovery of an archive of inscribed clay tablets by Italian excavators at Tell Mardikh (Ebla) in Syria, dating between about 2500 and 2300 BC, even earlier supposed datings of a 'Patriarchal period' were suggested. These new texts, the oldest yet found in Syro-Palestine, were said to be written in the 'proto-Canaanite' language, when not in Sumerian (9). Moreover, they were said to contain many place-names identical with those in the Biblical account of the Patriarchs as given in *Genesis*. More careful study and mature reflection revealed that the local language of Ebla ('Eblaite'), though definitely semitic (unlike Sumerian), was not so easily classified and, anyway, the place-names were not those given in the Bible.

The most vulnerable aspects of the 'Amorite migration hypothesis' have often been scrutinised in recent years, particularly by historians. In the first place, the text of the Old Testament does not present the Patriarchs as part of such an influx, nor do the Egyptian 'Execration Texts', and other sources identify the wandering Asiatics of Southern Palestine either as Amorites or as peoples recently arrived there. At the same time it has been made clear that the Mesopotamian texts have no direct relevance to the situation in Palestine in the centuries on either side of 2000 BC. The Amorite-speaking peoples were then primarily to be found along the line of the River Euphrates in eastern and northern Syria and east of the Middle Tigris in Iraq, but not south of Damascus. Furthermore, archaeologists now interpret breaks in the sequence of levels in excavated Palestinian mounds about 2350–2000 BC and earlier, as the result of internal factors that required no major change in population to put them into motion.

Other once popular arguments for dating the 'Patriarchal period' to the Middle Bronze Age (*c.* 1900–1550 BC) have also been discredited in the last few years. Comparisons of Patriarchal personal names, tribal names, laws and social customs with those recorded in archives of cuneiform tablets from the eighteenth-century BC royal palace at Mari, on the Middle Euphrates in modern Syria, or from the later fifteenth- and fourteenth-century private archives found in the provincial city of Nuzi, east of the River Tigris in modern Iraq, are no longer believed to have any chronological relevance. Too often either the Biblical or the extra-Biblical evidence had to be forced to make the comparison convincing and even then it might be so general as to apply with equal force to the first millennium BC.

Among the scholars who wished to identify and date a 'Patriarchal period', yet rejected the Middle Bronze Age as the most likely time for it, there were a number who sought to place it much closer to the entry of the Israelites into Canaan in the centuries on either side of 1200 BC. Then, it was argued, the majority of acknowledged anachronisms in the *Genesis* narrative, so embarrassing to advocates of an earlier 'Amorite' setting for the Patriarchs,

Above **8** View of Tell Mardikh in Syria (ancient Ebla) from the south-west. In the left background is the acropolis with the third-millennium palace, whence came the famous archive of tablets. In the foreground is the lower city. The Italian excavations here are directed by Matthiae.

Below **9** Clay tablets inscribed, in the cuneiform script, in the Eblaite and the Sumerian languages, as found in 1975 along the east wall of the Archive Room in the Royal Palace, *c.* 2500–2350 BC, at Tell Mardikh (Ebla) in Syria by the Italian excavators. They had presumably fallen in order when the wooden shelves on which they were stored had disintegrated. This is the oldest archive yet discovered in Syro-Palestine.

10 An intact male burial at Jericho of the type characterised by Kathleen Kenyon as 'Dagger Tombs', from the single such copper-bronze weapon placed with the body. She associated these men with an 'Amorite' invasion of Palestine, from the east or north-east, in the late third millennium BC.

disappear, since they are appropriate to the early part of the Iron Age. But even then elements remain in the Biblical text as we have it, not least the Mesopotamian background for the early chapters of *Genesis*, that more probably reflect the preoccupations and attitudes of an editor, or editors, living after the Babylonian Exile of the earlier sixth century BC (see below).

Such academic uncertainty will perhaps baffle the layman, but it offers a striking illustration of the acute difficulty and complexity of establishing the proper relationship between the Old Testament (as it has survived into modern times), extra-Biblical texts, and the mute information provided by excavations. It is important in this connection to remember that there are virtually no extra-Biblical texts of sufficient direct relevance to test the Old Testament's value as a reliable historical source in the period before about 900 BC, the opening of the Divided Monarchy. From that point the Biblical text may increasingly be supplemented, and its historical content thereby controlled, by extra-Biblical inscriptions of a historical character found in excavations throughout the Near East in the past one hundred and fifty years of archaeological investigation. It was over-optimistic interpretations of indirectly relevant texts from excavations at places like Ebla, Mari and Nuzi, to name but the best known, that bolstered the case of those who believed that a 'Patriarchal period' might be dated sometime in the Bronze Age. The nature of the text of the Old Testament does not lend itself to such simplistic historical analysis.

Historians in all ages have worked with conceptual models, in antiquity no less than today. There is good reason to think that the Biblical explanation of the emergence of Israel is precisely that. The model in this case is of a single extended family whose early history passes through successive chronological phases: the Patriarchs and the stay in Egypt; the Exodus and the conquest; the period of the Judges and the early kings. It is generally argued that this model evolved through the theological preconceptions of the post-Exilic writers and editors of the Old Testament. It was their concepts and purposes that combined older documents of various dates into the amalgam that we now read. In other words, the surviving text of the

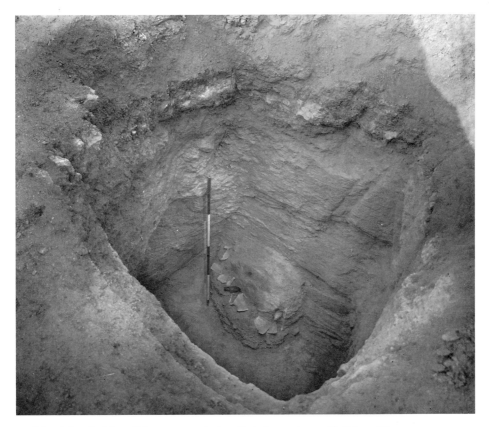

11 A burial at Jericho of the same period as that shown in 10. Kathleen Kenyon described tombs of this type as 'Pottery Tombs', since they contained no weapons but groups of little pottery jars and usually a four-spouted baked clay lamp placed in a niche. She believed they were also the graves of 'Amorite' intruders.

Old Testament, for all save the ultra-conservative or fundamentalist school of historians, is as 'stratified' as any of the mounds excavated by archaeologists. Analysing specific Biblical passages through form, source or tradition criticism is, then, no more, or less, subjective than interpreting a small area in a tell excavation. Both textual analysts and archaeologists must sift and critically assess their data.

We may only use a specific Biblical passage for historical purposes when we have established its editorial history, particularly the date of its earliest elements. This remains a formidable task. When historians or archaeologists have tried to employ Biblical texts wholly or even in part composed in the post-Exilic period, though purporting to describe much earlier events, as if they were of the same evidential value as an extra-Biblical inscription that certainly dates to that early period, confusions and misconceptions have inevitably followed.

3. Canaan in the Bronze Age

In the Old Testament 'Canaan' refers to the limited area where the Canaanites lived (cf. *Numbers* 13:29), 'land of Canaan' to a broader region. Here, as generally in modern scholarly literature, Canaan is used to describe the whole of the region west of the Jordan to the coast, southwards into Sinai and the Negev, northwards into the southern parts of modern Syria and the Lebanon. The Canaanites were seen by the writers of the Old Testament as the majority of the population in this area when the children of Israel penetrated it. The word may well denote a culture rather than a distinct ethnic or linguistic group, since the Biblical listing of Canaanites along with Amorites, Hittites, Hivites, Jebusites and others serves to emphasise the great ethnic and linguistic diversity of this relatively small area. This is an important fact, too easily overlooked in simplistic explanations of change in the region.

In recent years there have been no spectacular archaeological discoveries in Canaan from the Early and Middle Bronze Ages (*c.* 3000–1500 BC); but there has been a steady flow of new information and many critical re-appraisals of old knowledge that have radically modified previous explanations of cultural change during this time. These turn primarily on Canaan's diverse population and her pivotal position as a bridge both between Egypt and Western Asia, and between the east Mediterranean coast and the overland routes deep into Asia. When relating archaeological discoveries to the realities of daily life in the ancient landscapes of Palestine it has always to be remembered that not only was the population ethnically and linguistically heterogeneous, but it also formed an everchanging kaleidoscope of settled farmers and semi-nomadic pastoralists, of city-dwellers and peasants. It was never a static, homogeneous body of people only changed from time to time by sharp devastating intrusions from beyond its borders. Migrations and invasions there certainly were; but, as the best known one is to all intents and purposes archaeologically invisible, greater caution than has been customary in the past is needed when invoking them as explanations of the breaks or marked changes in the material record revealed by excavations. As Professor Franken has noted: 'the archaeologist would be totally unaware

12 Map of Canaan.

of any important ethnic changes at the end of the Late Bronze Age (see chapters 4–5) were it not for the biblical tradition.'

It is possible that the core of Canaan's population, and the primary local languages, were established there by the outset of the period known to archaeologists as the Bronze Age (*c*. 3000 BC). This is the time when the first pharaohs emerged in Egypt, ruling over a unified state with a complex administrative organisation that united religious and secular authority, with a very distinctive material culture and with its own writing system (hiero-glyphic). To the east of Canaan, in the region between the rivers Euphrates and Tigris (Mesopotamia), independent Sumerian city-states with a com-parable level of organisation and material achievement, and with their own method of writing (cuneiform), struggled for control over one another. Largely dependent on the peripheral mountain regions for valued raw materials, they drove deep into Syria and Iran, stimulating political and economic development there. By the middle of the third millennium BC scribes in the major cities of Syria were using the Sumerian language and writing down their local languages in borrowed cuneiform script, as illustrated by the remarkable archives of tablets found in the 1970s in the palace at Ebla (Tell Mardikh). But to the south the land of Canaan was still strictly speaking 'prehistoric', despite links with Egypt in one direction, Syro-Mesopotamia in the other.

At this time (the Early Bronze Age, *c*. 3000–2350 BC) in Palestine and parts of Jordan open settlements with comparatively sparse populations gave way to enclosed concentrations of people settled in one place for long periods of time. These early towns had impressive walls and gates, complex cemeteries, temples and other public buildings, as at Arad and Bab ed-Dhra in the south, at Ai and Jericho in the centre, at Megiddo and Beth-Yerah (Khirbet Kerak) in the north. In the countryside, with which these early towns were intimately linked, husbandry, particularly sheep- and goat-rearing, was combined with gradually intensifying cultivation of such agri-cultural produce as barley and wheat, grapes and olives, in much the same pattern as survived into modern times.

From sometime about 2350 BC (Early Bronze IV or Early to Middle Bronze Age) there was a marked recession in urban life, with destructions at different times on major town sites, for reasons not yet fully understood. Archae-ological surveys in recent years in the arid regions on the periphery of Canaan, in the desert fringes of eastern Transjordan, in the Golan Heights, and southwards into the Negev and Sinai have revealed at this time many ephemeral settlements in the open, and the use of cave-dwellings. Extensive cemeteries at places like Dhahr Mirzbaneh and Ein Samiyeh and Jericho, where there is no sign of corresponding contemporary permanent settle-ment, indicate a widely disseminated nomadic and semi-nomadic population living in simple, scattered and short-lived settlements. Craft industries flourished such as pottery and metalworking. Where the archaeological record indicates outside contacts, they are now with the north and north-east rather than with Egypt.

At this time both the Egyptian delta and parts of western Mesopotamia were subject to unusual pressure from pastoralist infiltration; but where surviving texts assist modern explanations, it may be seen that the native population absorbed the newcomers, and established institutions largely survived. It is in the light of this interpretation that scholars now increasingly see the situation in Canaan. There, too, infiltration and adoption may be closer to the truth than invasion and migration. As was mentioned in the previous chapter, previous conceptions of a major invasion at this period of nomadic Amorite-speaking peoples from the east and north-east, displacing and largely replacing the earlier urban-based peoples of Canaan, now seem exaggerated. A more complex, subtle process of innovation and adaptation is currently argued. Disruptive, if minor, climatic variations, the collapse of commercial networks with Egypt particularly, and population pressures from outside may best explain the interruption for three hundred years or more on urban sites after about 2350 BC.

13 A uniquely well-preserved Middle Bronze Age mud-brick city gate at Tel Dan excavated by Biran in 1979–80 in the south-west corner of the mound. The original archway was 3.6 m high; it is 5.15 m wide. Steps lead up to the archway which is flanked on either side by a slightly projecting tower.

By 2000–1900 BC, at the outset of the Middle Bronze Age, urban settlements slowly revived, probably under economic and social stimulus from the north, where the urban recession had been neither so marked nor so enduring. The period from about 1800–1550 BC was to be one of unusual prosperity for the major towns of Canaan, and one of the most remarkable phases in its history. Unthreatened by their neighbours to north, east or west, but in prosperous commercial contact with them, the rich upper-class Canaanite town-dwellers flourished.

Around the seventeenth century BC, as isolated, brief inscriptions from Gezer, Tell ed-Duweir (Lachish) and Shechem make clear, the Canaanites developed a literacy of their own that was to be of universal significance. Unknown men, perhaps one man alone, in circumstances of persisting obscurity then conceived the idea of the alphabet; an abstraction and simplification in writing that required less than thirty signs as against the hundreds used in the complex writing systems then used in Egypt and Mesopotamia. It is the direct ancestor of our own writing system and the Canaanites' greatest contribution to western civilisation. The 'Proto-Canaanite' script, a picture writing, was most probably conceived under the influence of Egyptian hieroglyphs; but the Canaanites reduced them to a mere twenty-seven new signs with their stance depending on the direction of writing, which was still flexible. Each sign represented a consonant plus any vowel. The script emerged in south Canaan, but its mechanical aspects were borrowed directly from Egyptian scribes then active in the region for economic rather than for political reasons.

Excavations have steadily revealed more and more about the period in which this remarkable innovation appeared. The Middle Bronze Age towns had been made familiar before 1939 by excavations on such major mounds as Tell el-Ajjul, Tell Beit Mirsim, Jericho and Megiddo. The re-emergence of towns after the recession of the later third millennium BC has recently been studied, particularly in a series of excavations in the coastal area at Akko, Poleg, Yavneh-Yam and Zeror. At Aphek especially a stratigraphic sequence from the later Early Bronze Age right through to the mature Middle Bronze Age has elucidated this critical transition. As at other sites, like Dan, Gezer, Hazor and Jericho, it is now clear that Aphek's formidable defensive system goes back in conception to the beginning of the period; indeed their precursors are to be found in the Early Bronze Age. Field research has also penetrated to regions not previously investigated, as at Dan and Hazor in Galilee, at Shechem and Tell el-Farah (North) in the central highlands, at Malhata and Masos in the eastern Negev. At the same time ever more refined methods of surface surveying, followed by selective excavation, have revealed much more about the lesser settlements and isolated buildings so often ignored by the pioneers of archaeology in Canaan.

14 Aerial view of Hazor, excavated by Yadin, showing the bottle-shaped mound of the Upper City, to the south, in the foreground. It was the nucleus of the settlement on this site from the earliest occupation there through to the first millennium BC. Beyond it is the vast enclosure marking the Lower City, established sometime in the earlier second millennium BC (Middle Bronze Age), and occupied down to the early thirteenth century BC (towards the end of the Late Bronze Age).

Below **15** The irregular profile of Tell es-Sultan (ancient Jericho), excavated by Kenyon (1952–8), showing how erosion and modern excavation have altered its shape. Beyond is the oasis which first attracted settlers to the site in remote prehistory, and the mountains east of the River Jordan.

16 A modern artist's impression of the inhabitants and furnishings of a house at Jericho, *c.* 1800–1650 BC. This reconstruction is closely based on objects and skeletons found in rock-cut tombs of this period at Jericho. They remain unique for the range of organic materials (wood, basketry, food) preserved in them by freak natural conditions that inhibited the processes of decay encountered on other archaeological sites.

This has indicated a greater density of settlement in the coastal plain and something of a decline in the highlands and in Transjordan compared with the peak of Early Bronze Age settlement. Among the excavations on lesser towns those at Nahariyah, with an important shrine, and Mevorakh in the coastal plain, at Tel Kitan in the Beth-Shan valley, and at Givat Yeshayahu near Beth Shemesh in the Shephelah, are particularly instructive. This new work, as so often in Canaan, has revealed marked regional variations in material culture, notably in potting, between north and south, between the coastal plain and the interior.

Unique evidence of the household equipment of this time is provided by rock-cut tombs at Jericho, where freak physical conditions preserved organic materials normally long since decayed on other sites in Canaan (17). The Middle Bronze Age tombs at Jericho were quite unlike those of the preceding Early to Middle Bronze period. They had rock-cut shafts and chambers and were very clearly family vaults. As each member of the family was buried,

17 General view into the rock-cut tomb H.18 at Jericho as found during the Kenyon excavations there (one wooden table has been removed), dating *c.* 1800–1650 BC (cf. 16). On the right are the remains of a wooden bedstead, on the left a wooden table with a large wooden dish of the type upon which joints of meat were set; there is a well-preserved basket at the lower left.

the earlier remains and the accompanying grave-goods were pushed to the rear of the chamber to create a jumbled mound of bones and offerings. However, when the Middle Bronze Age town of Jericho came to an abrupt end the final burials of the period were not disturbed, since the families had no successors, and therefore the bodies and the accompanying offerings were intact. From these final tombs full evidence could be obtained of the burial practices. It was clear that the dead were buried with the furniture and possessions which they had acquired during life, and on this basis a reconstruction can be made of their household equipment. Inorganic materials appear regularly elsewhere in tombs, but at Jericho wooden furniture, vessels and combs, as well as rush baskets and matting, with traces of textiles and food offerings, have also survived.

Canaanite temples are best known from examples of the later Middle and Late Bronze Age (see below), but one famous religious monument of the earlier period has recently been restudied. Since its discovery by Macalister in 1902, the 'High Place' at Gezer has held a special place in the study of Canaanite religion, though its dating was controversial. It consists of ten stone monoliths set in a straight line from north to south, erected at the same time on a platform of undressed stones with a curb of boulders. At one point there is a large stone block set horizontally with cavities in the

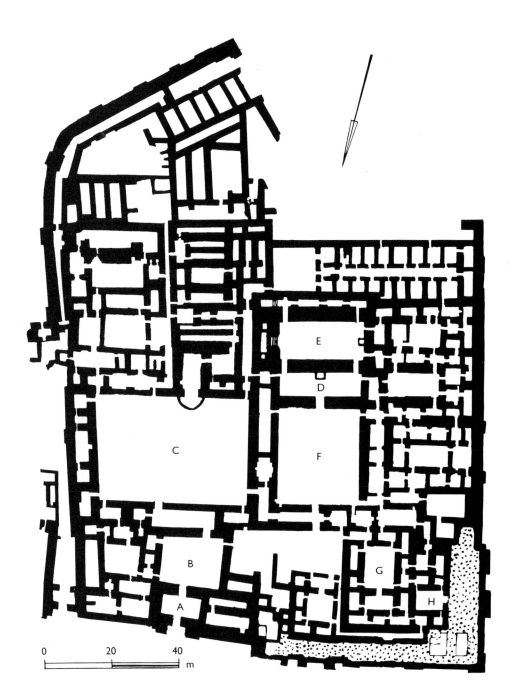

18 Diagrammatic ground plan of the excavated areas in the great mud-brick royal palace at Mari on the River Euphrates in modern Syria in the earlier second millennium BC, excavated by Parrot. The entrance was through A and B into the main public courtyard C; oblique entrances then led into the royal reception rooms (D and E) grouped round an inner court (F), with the more private royal accommodation, administrative quarters and scribal offices with archives beyond them to the west. It is noticeable how much thicker the external defensive wall is in the corner, protecting G and H.

top, commonly called an 'altar'. In fresh American excavations from 1967 to 1971 at Gezer this structure was found to date to the later Middle Bronze Age, though it remained in use through the Late Bronze Age. The meaning of such sanctuaries remains uncertain. They may have been more common in Canaan than survivors indicate, perhaps providing the pattern for *Joshua* 4,9: 'Then Joshua set up twelve stones in mid-Jordan ... they are there even now.'

Until very recently, and still in many books and articles, studies of the Bible and archaeology that deal with the evidence from the Middle Bronze Age, often indeed known as the 'Age of the Patriarchs' (chapter 2), paid much attention to the results of over fifty years of intermittent excavations by a French expedition at ancient Mari (Tell Hariri) on the Middle Euphrates in modern Syria. There almost the entire mud-brick royal palace of the later nineteenth and eighteenth centuries BC, covering some 2.5 hectares, has now been uncovered. Private royal apartments, public reception rooms, offices, kitchens, store-rooms and shrines were all enclosed within a circuit of defensive walls (18). Wall-paintings decorated some of the rooms and court-yards.

The heyday of the palace at Mari was under its most powerful king, Zimri-Lim, during the disturbed times accompanying the rise to power in Mesopotamia of Hammurabi of Babylon, who eventually sacked the palace, so preserving much of its material culture for the archaeologist. It has yielded a wealth of small finds, none so revealing as the palace archives. Well over 20,000 tablets are reported: letters of every kind, lists of personnel, records of legal decisions, of taxes, of supplies for the royal kitchens and ration distributions, as well as texts relevant to cults and rituals, mostly in the Akkadian (Babylonian) language written in the cuneiform script. The royal correspondence embraces a wide area, into Iran and the Gulf, into Assyria, and into Canaan, where Hazor and possibly Laish (Tel Dan) are mentioned in commercial texts, notably some showing the export westwards from Mari of tin for bronze-making.

It is probably no coincidence that it is in the mature Middle Bronze Age that the earliest known text written in Akkadian is reported from Canaan. It is still an isolated find, made at Hazor. Unfortunately, it was reported by a tourist, not from a controlled excavation, in 1962, and was published in 1974. It is the record of a legal decision.

The Mari texts revealed a significant number of Amorite-speaking people in the population of Mari and its surroundings. As this is a language related to those spoken in Canaan and later in Israel, there are valuable points of linguistic comparison. Moreover, whilst commerce was in the hands of city-dwellers, above all the royal family, farming and husbandry were handled by tribally organised semi-nomads in the semi-desert adjacent to the city.

They had a life-style similar to that attributed to the Patriarchs in the Old Testament. But this offers no grounds for dating the Patriarchs to this period, for this is simply the best Bronze Age textual evidence we have at present for a timeless way-of-life in the Near East, with equally long-lived social and family customs. When studying the tablets from Mari, or Ebla, or Ugarit, or for that matter from anywhere else, it is important to give equal weight to both the similarities and the dissimilarities with the Biblical account. If similarities alone are cited, the culture of Mari will inevitably seem more like that described in *Genesis* than in reality it was. Although scholars concerned with the origins of the Israelites now increasingly reject any direct historical connection between the Mari texts and the Biblical narratives, the Mari documents, rightly studied, still offer useful evidence for ways-of-life beyond the reach of the virtually textless archaeology of Middle Bronze Age Canaan.

There was no recognisable break in Canaanite culture at the outset of the period known to archaeologists as the Late Bronze Age (*c.* 1550–1200 BC). The political scene, however, soon changed with the spread of Egyptian control in Canaan resulting from the far-reaching campaigns of the pharaohs of the Eighteenth Dynasty and their conflicts in Syria. Here they challenged the Hittites, whose empire had its heart in central Turkey, and the kingdom of Mitanni, which spread across the north of modern Syria and Iraq.

For the last fifty years, since French excavations began there in 1929, the site of ancient Ugarit (Ras Shamra) on the Syrian coast, with its architecture, small finds and archives of tablets, has served as the pattern for the last major phase of Canaanite culture, particularly its religious aspects. The cults of the Canaanites were heavily abused by the writers of the Old Testament, in particular their god Baal. The texts from Ugarit do not offer a comprehensive survey of Canaanite religious belief, nor even of the religion and cult of Ugarit itself; but they give vivid glimpses of the main deities and the more important festivals, rites and sacrifices of one important city of Syro-Palestine around 1400–1300 BC. Continuing research steadily sifts out the material most relevant to Biblical study, since initial interpretations, as with the Mari texts, pressed many parallels too far. Religious practices and the range of deities in the cities of Canaan itself may not always have been directly comparable to those of Ugarit, but, wherever they may be checked, there is sufficient overlap to leave the Ras Shamra texts in a unique position until a major city in Palestine yields a comparable archive of tablets.

The texts from Ugarit have accumulated during fifty years of excavation, interrupted for a decade by the Second World War. The highlights of the post-war years have been excavations in the small Southern Palace (1954–5), with its archives; the archives of Rap'anu found in the residential quarter in 1956; excavations in the Northern Palace from 1968 and the discovery of

37

the 'House of Alabasters' in 1973. The steadily increasing body of texts includes examples not only in the previously unknown local language, today called 'Ugaritic', but also in Akkadian and Sumerian (the languages of Mesopotamia), in Egyptian and in Hittite (the language of the rulers of Turkey), in Hurrian (a language spoken in eastern Turkey and southwards into Syria and Mesopotamia) and in the local language of Cyprus. This indicates Ugarit's vital role as a commercial centre.

The language of Ugarit used an alphabetic script written in wedge-shaped (cuneiform) signs. This 'Ugaritic' alphabet was invented, apparently in the fifteenth or fourteenth century BC, indicating the impact of the Canaanite alphabet. The principle is that of the 'Proto-Canaanite' alphabet, but the means of writing – on clay tablets – was adopted from Akkadian, then the diplomatic language of the Near East. 'Ugaritic' alphabetic texts, all very short, have also been found at Sarepta in the Lebanon, and at Nahal Tavor, Taanach and Beth Shemesh in Israel, indicating that caution is still required in identifying it too closely with Ugarit just on account of the present concentration of finds there.

Knowledge of the religion of Ugarit comes from mythological texts, from lists of deities and sacrifices, and from other texts that may reflect rituals. The religion was polytheistic, with a pantheon of over thirty gods. It was an anthropomorphic religion, in which the gods exhibited all the human passions and frailties. Although there was a general pantheon, there was no uniformity; states and cities had their own special gods distinguished by individual epithets. El presided over the assembly of the gods as 'king', 'bull', 'father of mankind' or 'creator of creatures'. His wife was Athirat, associated with the sea, mother of the gods (cf. Asherah in 1 *Kings* 15:13; 18:19). Yam, Mot and Athtar are prominent among their children. Baal

'a b g ḫ d h w z ḥ ṭ v k š l

m ḏ n ẓ s ʿ p ṣ q r ṯ

ġ t 'i 'u s₂

19 The alphabet used at Ugarit (modern Ras Shamra), as written in a specially devised wedge-shaped (cuneiform) script on a clay tablet; perhaps a schoolboy's exercise. It shows the thirty Ugaritic signs written out in the order of the traditional Hebrew alphabet of twenty-two signs, with five extra letters (ḫ, š, d, ẓ, ġ), which subsequently became obsolete, and the addition of three others at the end ('i, 'u, and s₂).

was son of Dagan, not a member of El's family; indeed, he is often in opposition to them. This may not indicate real conflicts so much as Baal's coming to prominence at Ugarit at the time of the surviving texts, in the fifteenth and fourteenth centuries BC. Baal had numerous epithets: 'victor', 'lord', 'judge', 'rider of the clouds'; he was also identified with Hadad, a traditional Near Eastern storm-god. The warlike goddess Anat was regarded as his sister, variously known as 'wet-nurse of the gods' or 'sister-in-law of peoples'. Baal has rather different associations in the Old Testament, where he appears with Athirat (Asherah) or Athtarat (Ashtoreth: I *Samuel* 31 : 10; I *Kings* 11 : 33), who occurs at Ugarit, but not prominently in known texts.

The primary role of Ugaritic texts in Biblical Studies at present is broadly twofold: first, their use of a previously unknown Semitic language closely related to Hebrew helps to elucidate Old Testament Hebrew, notably problematic vocabulary; second, in so far as they may be held to represent 'Canaanite' religion, they assist with assessments of Israel's debt to Canaanite ideology and imagery. On perhaps the most fascinating problem of all, the processes through which Yahweh came to be the complex deity of *Psalms* and other archaic passages in the Old Testament, the light thrown by the Ugaritic texts is far less penetrating. This is largely explained by persisting ignorance about Yahweh's original character. This complicates any attempt to elucidate his relation to El or even to Baal in remote antiquity. There are, in both cases, striking affinities, but no less marked differences.

We are on firmer ground in the relation between the Bible and archaeology when we turn south to review the archaeology of Palestine in the Late Bronze Age (*c.* 1550–1200 BC), for here at this time not only did the inhabitants of the region call themselves 'Canaanites', but so did foreigners. Moreover, it is, whatever attitude is taken to the historical relevance of *Genesis* and *Exodus*, the background to the coming of the Israelites and the Philistines, who did so much to transform the region in the last two centuries of the second millennium BC. Recent archaeological surveys have shown that Canaan of the Late Bronze Age was more sparsely inhabited than in the great days of the later Middle Bronze Age. Unfortified villages in the highland areas appear to have disappeared, as permanent settlements were concentrated in more fertile lowland regions.

The city of Hazor, excavated by Yadin from 1955–8, continues to dominate the archaeological record at this time. At Hazor, as elsewhere in Canaan's major cities, the fine fortifications of the earlier period remained in use, emphasising continuity of location and culture. This is equally marked in the town's temples, which have added significantly to the documentation provided by temples in such important earlier excavations as those at Beth-Shan, at Tell ed-Duweir (Lachish), where the 'Fosse Temple' was particularly rich in small finds, at Megiddo and at Shechem. More

20 View of the Late Bronze Age shrine in area C at Hazor, with stone stelae and a seated stone statuette of a man or god still in position. One stela shows a pair of arms in a posture of worship. It is uncertain whether the statuette represents a deity or, perhaps more likely, a high-ranking man tendering perpetual respect to his gods.

recently excavations at Kamid el-Loz, in modern Lebanon, have revealed an important temple complex of this period with some features relevant to the study of Solomon's Temple (see chapter 6).

At Hazor six temples of the Late Bronze Age have been located in the area of the Lower City, only partly excavated, and there may well have been others. The plans have few common features, and there is not enough evidence to decide whether a particular plan was associated with a particular cult. In all temples, probably orientated to fit in with town planning, rites were performed in both the courtyard and the interior. The court was the place where the community could be involved in ceremonies like sacrifice and oracular consultations; the temple itself, as the 'house' of the deity, was often relatively small. Only the priests entered the temple proper, where priests' libations, sacrifices of animals and incense, and ritual meals took place. Vessels, censers and altars of incense have been found in shrines. Votive offerings were placed both in the porch and inside the temple; benches and platforms were built into temples to take them. So that they might not be profaned thereafter, votives were regularly cleared into pits to make way for new offerings. Divine symbols, whether stelae or statuary, were on a dais or in a niche near the centre-line of a shrine. Few have survived and some may well have been of precious or perishable materials, readily plundered or destroyed. Whether or not the divine presence was always screened off is not clear; but in certain cases this seems likely.

Two of Hazor's temples are especially interesting. One was a relatively small and simple structure in area C, built against the back of the earth bank that enclosed the Lower City. In a niche in one long wall of the single oblong chamber, with indirect entrance opposite, were set a stone statue of a seated male figure and a row of ten standing and one fallen stelae (20). Other stone slabs lay around. The statue had carved on its breast an inverted crescent, possibly identifying him as a moon-god, though he might be a royal human figure set here to honour the moon-god in perpetuity. One of the stelae was carved with two arms upraised, palms open, towards the symbol of a full moon, or possibly a sun-disk, set within a moon-crescent. Near this temple was found a silver-plated bronze cult standard decorated with a crescent, snakes and the figure of a deity. To the east of this shrine was a complex of pottery workshops, store-rooms and houses. Among the finds here was a small pottery mask (14 cm high), clean-shaven, with eye-cavities and holes in the perimeter for attachment. No wholly convincing hypothesis has yet been found for the purpose of this shrine or for the stelae, which are probably commemorative, rather than representative of deities.

A more important temple was excavated at the extreme north end of the Lower City at Hazor. The final version, destroyed in the thirteenth century

21 Aerial view of the Late Bronze Age temple in area H at Hazor. It is divided into three, as was Solomon's later temple in Jerusalem. From the left: entrance porch; central room; 'Holy of Holies', with a rear niche for the focus of worship, presumably in this case a fine statue of the main deity, long since destroyed or stolen.

BC, was very substantially built, in a tripartite plan, using large stone slabs (orthostats) to line the lower part of the inner walls in a manner best known from Hittite architecture in Turkey (21). Lion reliefs guarded either side of the entrance. In the inner room, the largest of the three and clearly the 'Holy of Holies', was found a remarkable group of cult objects for libations and offerings: a basalt incense altar, a basalt basin, two stone libation tables, two large baked clay jars, a basalt bowl decorated with a running spiral design and a stone offering table. Yadin suggested that a pottery vessel shaped like a house which was found here had perhaps been for holding the 'holy snakes of the temple'. A similar vessel found at Ugarit was actually decorated with the emblem of a snake. Here also were fine beads, seals of various types, metal statuettes and a small stone statue of a seated man or god, probably the former. This temple, sharing the same basic plan that was to be used centuries later for Solomon's Temple in Jerusalem, has given unusually varied information on the cult fittings of a Canaanite shrine.

Whereas Canaan was relatively isolated for most of the Middle Bronze Age, to judge by her material culture, the Late Bronze Age is, by contrast, characterised archaeologically by many imported objects, or local copies of them, found throughout the region and deep into Transjordan. The distinctive pottery of Cyprus and of the Aegean world (Mycenaean) was so popular that it largely displaced local fine wares, was widely imitated, and reduced local potters to a very routine repertory of shapes and decoration. Egyptian taste deeply influenced a growing production of luxury, largely cosmetic containers in glass, faience, and calcite or gypsum, whilst jewellery and seals in metal, glass and faience again followed Egyptian fashions. Luxury goods in perishable materials are known from texts, yet are very rarely retrieved in excavations. At Pella in Jordan, in 1984, Potts and the Australian Expedition found a set of beautifully carved ivory plaques *in situ*. Careful excavation allowed the later reconstruction of one of the wooden boxes to which they had once been fitted (22). The shape is distinctively Egyptian, as are the motifs; yet the style of the lions decorating the lid belongs to a non-Egyptian tradition, perhaps Canaanite.

At a time of widespread commercial contact in the east Mediterranean region it is not surprising that Canaan's coastal towns should have flourished, as is revealed by recent excavations at Akko, Ashdod and Shiqmonah. So also, for political as well as commercial reasons, did major centres on the route from Egypt into Syria. Some of the most notable among them, at sites like Tell el-Ajjul, Beth-Shan and Megiddo, were excavated in the pioneering days of Palestinian archaeology, but sites like Taanach and Pella, where work continues, have more recently increased knowledge of major cities in Late Bronze Age Canaan.

Until recently Palestine was regarded, in Albright's words, 'as an integral

22 Reconstructed wooden box, 13.6 cm high, with the original hippopotamus ivory inlays found by Australian excavators at Pella in Jordan in 1984. The inlays are carved in a derivative Egyptian style, though the shrine-like shape of the box is typically Egyptian. The lions are strongly reminiscent of the famous stone relief over the citadel gate at Mycenae in Greece, perhaps copied from designs on an imported Canaanite object similar to this Late Bronze Age box (*c.* 1650–1350 BC).

part of the Egyptian Empire' for the whole of the Late Bronze Age (*c.* 1550–1200 BC). New research has modified this view. The Egyptian connection at this time has long been of particular interest to Biblical scholars. Many of them have sought to set the background of the descent into Egypt and the influential position acquired by Joseph, in the period of Hyksos rule in Egypt, towards the end of the Middle Bronze Age, when Asiatics were dominant in the northern part of Egypt, as has been vividly illustrated by the excavations of Bietak and an Austrian team at Tell ed-Dab'a (? Avaris) in the eastern delta since 1966. Here parts of an extensive town, over what may previously have been an Egyptian royal summer residence, have been carefully excavated. It was largely inhabited by an Asiatic (Canaanite) population with their own distinctive variant of the material culture of Canaan in the mature Middle Bronze Age. In a different cultural environment and in relative isolation, they developed along their own lines. But numerous objects in both their houses and their graves are immediately recognisable as Canaanite rather than as Egyptian.

In fact, descents of nomadic Asiatics into the Egyptian delta from southern Canaan were commonplace, as is clear from texts and pictorial representation from Egypt over centuries from the third millennium BC onwards. Such movements were for commerce, to accommodate routine patterns of transhumance, or to pasture flocks in times of unusual climatic pressures. Memories of a descent into Egypt might have formed part of a clan or tribal oral record from any one of many such groups passing backwards and forwards from Canaan into Egypt during the Bronze Age. Nor, during the Late Bronze Age, were Asiatic prisoners-of-war, or others taken into captivity there, likely to have been rare among those forced to labour for Egyptian pharaohs on their public works. Whether or not Old Testament accounts of the 'Egyptian bondage' and the Exodus, are historically reliable, such events would not be out of place in this context.

Whatever the extent of Egyptian military destruction in southern and inland Canaan after the expulsion of the Asiatic Hyksos rulers from Egypt in the sixteenth century BC, and it may have been considerable, it is now largely agreed that the first organisation of Canaan into a political and commercial empire under Egypt's domination falls a century or so later, under Tuthmosis III (*c.* 1479–1425 BC), whose campaigns in the East are among the best documented in Egyptian history. Following them, towns in western Canaan controlling the coastal route, and in the north guarding Egypt's route into Syria, began to flourish as the principal suppliers of food and other needs for the military enterprises and local administration undertaken by Egyptians in the following two centuries.

This is the so-called 'Egyptian Peace', so vividly documented in the famous Amarna Letters, found a century ago at Tell el-Amarna in central Egypt, where they had been stored in the middle years of the fourteenth century BC in the archive of the 'heretic' pharaoh Akhenaten. He was married to the renowned Queen Nefertiti and may, by another wife, have been Tutankhumun's father. In this archive were letters to the Pharaoh from client rulers of city-states in Canaan, composed in a form of the Akkadian language, including actual Canaanite words, and written on clay tablets in the cuneiform script. In Canaan itself only one such archive has yet been found. At Taanach, early this century, the German excavators recovered seven tablets and five fragments. But slowly, year by year, scattered finds of Akkadian texts from Canaan have come to total some forty examples, notable among them recent finds at Hazor and Aphek (25).

It is in the Amarna Letters that the controversial Ḥabiru (*'Apiru*) are to be found as a troublesome element in the population of Canaan. There is still no general agreement over what, if any, connection there was between these social and political misfits and the Biblical Hebrews. Where once close identity was seen, there is now more scepticism among scholars. Nor is it now believed that Egypt lost its grip on Canaan at this time in the mid-fourteenth century BC. Egypt had problems, but it is far from certain that they seriously impaired her ability to exercise effective control where it mattered to her in Canaan.

In the thirteenth and earlier twelfth centuries BC, however, both textual

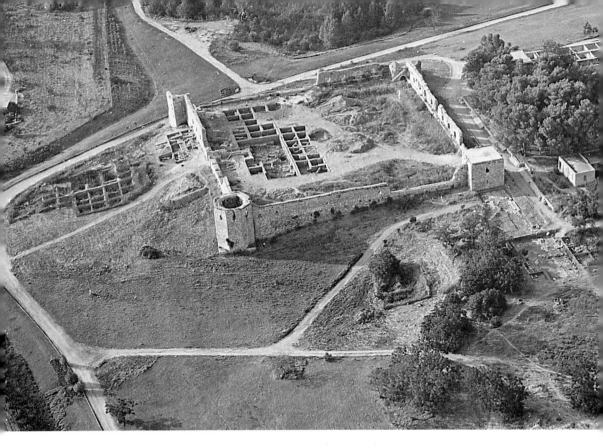

23 Aerial view of the excavations at Aphek-Antiparis, directed by Kochavi and Beck, partly within the walls of a relatively modern Ottoman Turkish fort. This shows the continuing occupation of a site in a favourable natural and strategic location.

and archaeological evidence may now increasingly be seen to indicate that Egypt sharply tightened her military control, with increased numbers of Egyptian army and administrative personnel established in Canaan. In this phase more of almost every type of Egyptian object, and distinctive types of Egyptian architecture, as at Beth-Shan and Tells Farah (South), Hesi, Jemmeh, Masos and esh-Sharia, appear in Palestine than in any comparable period in the Bronze Age. What effect the intensified Egyptian occupation had on urban and rural life in Canaan is very hard to gauge archaeologically; what indications there are suggest that it was harsh.

Culturally the profound impact of Egyptian fashions and styles is everywhere apparent to the extent that mature Canaanite art is now largely recognised through its Egyptianising traits. It was an eclectic art, however, borrowing from many foreign sources, Egypt only the most evident amongst them, yet it was capable of expressing in the relatively few really fine objects to have survived a distinctive style of its own that was ancestral to the more familiar art of Phoenicia in later centuries.

At Timna in the south the Egyptians exploited the local copper mines in

45

24 A 'Proto-Canaanite' inscription on a fragment of limestone (an ostracon) from a twelfth-century BC village at Izbat Sartah, 3 km east of Aphek-Antiparis. It was probably incised by a semi-literate person, who first wrote out the local linear alphabet (cf. 19) and then either random letters or a text not yet understood by modern scholars.

collaboration with the Midianites, who came from east of the Red Sea, and other local tribesmen. Here, as for centuries in the mines of Serabit el-Khadim in Sinai, Egyptians and Asiatics worked together under the patronage of the Egyptian goddess Hathor, whose small temple at Timna has yielded numerous votive offerings, some inscribed. These suggest a major period of exploitation from at least the reign of Seti I (*c.* 1306–1290 BC) to that of Ramses V (*c.* 1156–1151 BC). A particularly distinctive type of painted pottery from Timna and other sites in the Negev occasionally penetrated further north and has now been termed 'Midianite' after its probable creators.

Although texts in Akkadian, Ugaritic or Egyptian continue to dominate the record of documentary finds made by archaeologists in Canaan during the Late Bronze Age, sufficient finds have been made in the last few decades to refine understanding of the complex history of the local alphabet, whose ultimate origin has already been noted. In the thirteenth century BC local writing of the south Canaanite dialect had reduced the numbers of alphabetic signs it used to twenty-two. In the following two centuries these linear signs developed into clearly formed letters and the direction of writing stabilised, so that from about the eleventh century BC it was set out in horizontal lines from right to left. It is about this point that scholars refer to this script as 'Phoenician' rather than as 'Proto-Canaanite', its name in the Bronze Age.

Among recent finds in the transitional stage is an ostracon dated to the twelfth century BC from Izbat Sartah, a village just inland from Aphek. This sherd is faintly inscribed with over eighty signs (24). It is generally agreed that the first row is a faulty rendering of the twenty-two-letter 'Proto-Canaanite' alphabet. Controversy surrounds the remaining four lines, which do not seem to render a coherent text and are possibly the work of a semi-literate person. As in Egypt at this time, it is likely that papyrus was already the normal writing material for any text of significance, and papyrus is particularly subject to destruction. Only drafts, banal messages and exercises are likely to have been written or scratched on pieces of pot, stone or bone, so caution has to be exercised in assessing what they reveal of a people's literacy. But it is possible that the simplicity of the alphabet, even at this

25 Clay tablet excavated at Aphek, inscribed in the cuneiform script of Mesopotamia in the Akkadian language of that region used for international diplomatic correspondence. It is a letter from the ruler of Ugarit on the coast in north Syria to a high-ranking Egyptian official, presumably resident at Aphek, in the time of Ramses II of Egypt (*c.* 1290–1224 BC) or soon thereafter.

early date, allowed for a degree of literacy greater than was possible either in Egypt or Mesopotamia, where complex writing systems could only be mastered by professional scribes jealous of the power literacy gave them.

The role of Egypt in Canaan and her wider contacts towards the end of the Late Bronze Age have been particularly clearly illustrated by Kochavi's work since 1972 at Tel Aphek, near the source of the River Sharon. Here the Canaanite acropolis has been located beneath the courtyard of an Ottoman fort (23). Several superimposed public buildings have now been excavated. The earliest may have been a royal palace in the sixteenth century BC; the latest, possibly the residence of a governor responsible to Egypt, is a square building extending across some 500 square metres. Only the basement level was extant, a fire sometime in the second half of the thirteenth century had destroyed the structure. The upper storey(s) had collapsed into the lower, bringing down a remarkable collection of small finds in addition to bricks and painted plaster, carbonised wooden beams and building stones. Many items in the pottery repertory were distinctively Egyptian.

Among the fragmentary inscriptions were a type of Sumerian/Akkadian dictionary common among scribes writing Akkadian in the cuneiform script on clay tablets; a trilingual Sumerian/Akkadian/Canaanite dictionary, the first such in which the third language was Canaanite; and a fragmentary clay seal impression bearing a royal name in the hieroglyphic script used by the Hittites. Most significant of all, however, was a complete letter in Akkadian from the ruler of Ugarit to a high Egyptian official, presumably resident in the building at Aphek, in the reign of Ramses II (*c.* 1290–1224 BC) or soon after (25). Above the ruins of this building, in an Iron Age context, was found a tiny faience plaque (2.5 × 4 cm) of a type usually associated in Egypt with foundation deposits in temples. It was inscribed on both sides in ink, in Egyptian hieroglyphic script, with the name of Ramses II and a dedication to the Egyptian goddess Isis, who may have had a temple in Aphek.

Excavations in Canaan and elsewhere in recent years have not significantly elucidated the earliest phase in the existence of Israel. The well-known inscribed stela of the pharaoh Merneptah (*c.* 1224–1214 BC), set up in the fifth year of his reign, remains of critical importance for any historical reconstruction. It is still, after a century and a half of serious archaeological

Right **26** and **27** Drawing of reliefs (inscription omitted) on a temple wall at Karnak in Egypt. They have long been attributed to the time of the Egyptian pharaoh Ramses II (*c.* 1290–1224 BC). Yurco has recently suggested that they should be attributed to the reign of Merneptah (*c.* 1224–1214 BC) and linked to the famous 'Israel Stela' carved in his time. **26** (*above*) shows the siege of Ashkelon, and **27** (*below*) may show the defeat of the people of Israel as related in Merneptah's 'Israel Stela'.

research, the only monument with a specific mention of 'Israel' in ancient Egyptian records and by far the earliest attestation of the name in an extra-Biblical source. As its witness to the presence of a people bearing this name in Canaan at the end of the thirteenth century BC is crucial to all hypotheses about the Exodus, the Wandering and the settlement in Canaan, any fresh information relating to it is unusually significant.

The very rhetorical style of the poem in which the key phrase occurs has always complicated study of it:

Canaan has been plundered into every sort of woe:
Ashkelon
has been overcome;
Gezer has been captured
Yano'am is made non-existent.
Israel is laid waste and his seed is not.

It has recently been persuasively argued by Yurco that four battle scenes carved on a temple wall at Karnak in Egypt, long attributed to Ramses II, in fact illustrate the victories mentioned by Merneptah on the 'Israel Stela'. In these reliefs three fortified cities are shown under assault (certainly Ashkelon (26), and what are assumed to be Gezer and Yano'am) and then a group of Asiatic people defeated in open battle, presumably 'Israel' (27); the word is written on the stela in Egyptian hieroglyphs with the sign indicating a people rather than a land. Clearly the Egyptians did not regard Israel at this time as a city-state like Ashkelon or Gezer, but as a distinct group of people not named after a particular city or territory. Interestingly, unlike other cities and foreign countries when written in Egyptian, 'Israel' is masculine not feminine, perhaps associating it with a male deity or heroic founding figure. The south-to-north order of the three city-states in Merneptah's poem does not offer decisive directions for locating 'Israel' within Canaan at this time.

This isolated incident tells us little or nothing about the events through which Canaan passed gradually into eclipse as it was threatened from both land and sea, and as the power of Egypt steadily retreated, from the earlier twelfth century BC. This complex process, perhaps the most controversial in the whole relationship between Biblical sources and archaeology, is the subject of the next two chapters.

4. The eclipse of Canaan
I: The Egyptians and the Philistines

As we approach through archaeology the period during which the people of Israel settled in Canaan it is important to bear in mind that this critical series of events, upon which the Old Testament is naturally insistent, was only one aspect in a complex process of social and military action over a period of two hundred years, from about 1200/1150 to 1000/950 BC. As Egyptian authority in Canaan, so effective in the later phases of the Late Bronze Age, passed into eclipse, it left a power vacuum in certain places that had profound consequences. The most immediate beneficiaries of this retreat were the Philistines and their close associates, some of whom had probably first entered the towns of western Canaan as mercenaries in the Egyptian service. Study of their material culture has been a major aspect of archaeological research in Israel in recent years.

Nor should the Canaanite city-states themselves be overlooked. Many of them endured long as political, economic and cultural centres, whilst their artistic traditions and religious life had a vitality and tenacity that persisted into the Iron Age, profoundly affecting the development of society in Israel, Judah and Philistia. This was a period of assimilation and adaptation, not of replacement; significant Canaanite populations endured in many areas.

To some extent independent of the social and political changes of the time was the advent in the twelfth century of the use of iron for tools and weapons: the diagnostic feature that archaeologists have traditionally taken as the material mark of change at this time. A few iron objects, usually no more than trinkets in Palestine, but more substantial in Hittite centres in Syria and Turkey, had certainly been made in the Late Bronze Age, but no major iron-production centres are yet archaeologically apparent then. Although traditionally associated with the Philistines, the appearance of manufactured iron in Canaan may have had a more complex history. It certainly involved the intrusive Philistines and their associates, who had links with pioneer ironworking in Cyprus, Syria and Turkey, but also the Canaanites and Israelites.

With pottery, as with ironwork, it is now clear that the presence or absence of particular types in specific excavations is insufficient basis on which to

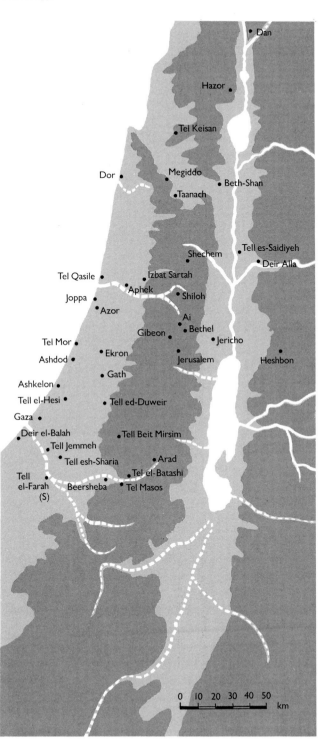

28 Map of Canaan at the
time of the arrival of the
'Sea Peoples' and the
Israelites, *c.* 1200–1000 BC.

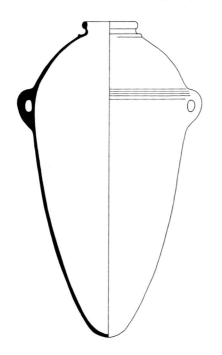

29 Drawing of a 'collared-rim' jar, a type of pottery storage jar, long taken to be particularly distinctive of the early Iron Age, *c*. 1200–1100 BC, and associated by many scholars with intrusive Israelites. It had, in fact, appeared earlier, if rarely, and even at its greatest use may not be exclusively linked to the incoming Israelites.

establish chronological arguments or ethnic associations. It is the quantitative relationships between various pottery types that must first be carefully established and then only be explained in terms of specific peoples with great caution. At the transition from the Bronze Age to the Iron Age pottery changed slowly. A particular type of storage jar, named after its distinctive rim as the 'collared-rim' jar, has long been taken as particularly distinctive of the early Iron Age and closely associated with the intrusive Israelites. It does indeed become most common then, but it had occurred sporadically before, as at sites like Aphek in the coastal plain. In general, the legacy of Canaan's Bronze Age potters may be detected to a greater or lesser extent in the ceramics used on all the earliest settlements attributed both to the Israelites and the Philistines.

Perhaps no period in the historic range of archaeology in Palestine has so much benefited from the techniques of surface surveying as has Iron Age I (twelfth to tenth centuries BC). The growing significance of systematic field surveys in the development of archaeological research in the last twenty years, following the pioneering work of Nelson Glueck from the 1930s through into the 1950s, has already been mentioned. It was he who, using the pottery typologies and chronologies worked out by Albright, demonstrated how patterns of settlement could be mapped out through time by study of the pottery sherds found on the surface of ancient sites, particularly in Jordan and the Negev.

This was, initially, a technique particularly used in peripheral or desert regions, but it has subsequently proved equally revealing elsewhere. Its value has been greatly enhanced in the last thirty years by the use of teams of specialists from many disciplines both to gather and to process the data. Attention is now concentrated on small areas, so as to give as much consideration to the natural history of the landscape through time as to the history of its exploitation by man. It has also been realised more recently that the identification and dating of pottery, both in Syro-Palestine and Transjordan, must make special note of marked regional variations. Checking and rechecking survey results through trial excavations at carefully selected sites is vital. Such work also helps to confirm the diverse functions of sites identified only from surface debris – isolated farms, forts, villages, etc. – since this knowledge is vital for any social or economic interpretation of results.

It is this rapid development of surface survey in recent years, not least because it is so cost-effective, that has switched attention in archaeology from an almost exclusive concentration on major tells, usually those whose Biblical identity was reasonably well established, to the landscape in which they were situated and of which, in antiquity, they had been an intimate part. Archaeologists now study these sites as parts of functioning political, social and economic systems set in specific natural settings with complex histories and characters of their own.

This change of perspective has had a particularly sharp impact on the study of the emergence of Israel in Canaan, and it clearly indicates that this process was primarily a rural phenomenon. The most effective contribution of archaeological research towards understanding how Israel came to supersede Canaan between the twelfth and tenth centuries BC, whilst withstanding the Philistine challenge, is likely to be in the general picture of towns and villages, farms and forts, cult places and ritual centres, all interacting in a landscape. The approach which compares the particular, and possibly exceptional, stratigraphic sequences in a few widely scattered major towns is one which, as will be seen below, led scholars studying the relationship between the Biblical narratives concerning Israel's entry into Canaan and the archaeological evidence into a series of apparent contradictions. Even though the modern state of Israel has now been more intensively surveyed than any other comparable region of the Near East, the same problems apply to the interpretation of results as elsewhere.

At this point it is necessary to examine the state of Canaan at the crucial time, in the late thirteenth and earlier twelfth centuries BC. In archaeological terms this is the transition from the Late Bronze Age to the early Iron Age. Excavations in the last fifteen to twenty years on sites in Canaan and across northern Sinai into the Egyptian Delta have increasingly indicated that the once popular concept of a single concentrated wave of destructions sweeping Canaanite culture into oblivion in the later thirteenth or early twelfth century BC was misconceived. Although certain towns, such as Bethel and Hazor were indeed destroyed sometime between 1300 and 1200 BC, they may well have been the exception rather than the rule. Numerous other towns in Canaan enjoyed continuity of occupation at this time and some enjoyed considerable prosperity. The primary crisis is now seen to have occurred some generations later, with the final collapse of Egyptian rule during or soon after the reign of the Egyptian pharaoh Ramses VI (c. 1151–1143 BC). He is the last pharaoh whose name is clearly associated with Egyptian activity in the mines at Serabit el-Khadim in Sinai and at Timna in the Negev. There had been intermittent troubles earlier in the century, but textual evidence suggests that Ramses III (c. 1194–1163 BC) had restored some degree of Egyptian control. At its most effective Egyptian power had operated from key centres in and around Gaza, at Joppa further up the coast, probably at Aphek in the Sharon Plain, and at Beth-Shan in the Plain of Esdraelon. These were major administrative centres with garrisons of troops, including peoples other than native Egyptians, 'Philistines' amongst them.

In the present archaeological record the marks of this final intensive phase of Egyptian hegemony are unusually strong, not, as so often before, only confined to the evidence of small Egyptian objects. At Ashdod and at Joppa fragments of door-jambs from city gates, at Beth-Shan thresholds, door jambs and architraves, and at places like Lachish and Megiddo columns and capitals, are carved from stone in the distinctive Egyptian style. At Ashdod, Joppa and perhaps also at Lachish, inscribed fragments of stone or metal from city gates emphasise the Egyptian character of major public buildings, whilst a recently discovered temple at Lachish, and some discovered years ago at Beth-Shan, owe much to Egyptian architectural design.

More striking in this respect, because more widely distributed at present, are a series of large secular buildings typical in plan, and to some extent in construction, of Egyptian domestic architecture. Examples of these so-called 'Egyptian governors' residencies', or closely related structures, have now been excavated at Tells Farah (South), Hesi, Jemmeh and esh-Sharia in the strategically critical region within reach of Gaza, at Tel Masos in the Beersheva Valley, and northwards at Aphek and at Beth-Shan along the main route into Syria and Transjordan. They are square buildings of brick, without stone foundations, which conform to no single blue-print. Generally, small rooms are arranged round a central court, with an interior stairway and a corner entrance.

It is less easy to establish archaeologically how such centres operated. One series of finds has been unusually instructive in this respect. Excavations

30 A general view across the excavations at Tell esh-Sharia, directed by Oren, looking south. The 'Egyptian Residency' of the early twelfth century BC, in stratum IX, is marked by the wall stubs to the left. On the right, at a higher stratigraphical level, is a four-roomed house of the tenth to ninth centuries BC (stratum VII).

at Tell ed-Duweir (Lachish) in the 1930s had revealed ordinary pottery bowls inscribed on the inside in ink in the Egyptian hieratic script (a cursive form of hieroglyphs) with records of harvest taxes given in measures of grain, some dated 'Year 4' or 'Year 10' of an unnamed pharaoh (or pharaohs). In excavations at Tell esh-Sharia (30) in the Nahal Gerar (1972–8) Oren found many more such inscribed bowls listing substantial quantities of grain paid to the local temple or fort. The latest is dated to 'Year 20 + x', perhaps in the reign of Ramses III (*c*. 1194–1163 BC). As it is known from Egyptian texts that under Ramses III the tax income from parts of Canaan was granted to specific temples in Egypt, or to Egyptian temples in Canaan, these bowls may illustrate that system of collection in operation.

Surveys and limited excavations in northern Sinai in the last fifteen years have shown how this region was integrated into the Egyptian administrative and military system in the thirteenth and early twelfth centuries BC, with fortresses and granaries to provide for troop movements along the coastal road to and from Canaan. This vital artery sustained Egyptian authority in Canaan. A particularly vivid illustration of the impact of Egypt on a Canaan-

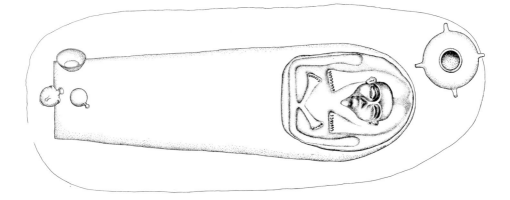

31 Drawing of an anthropoid baked clay coffin as found in tomb 116 at Deir el-Balah. Such distinctive coffins were once exclusively associated by scholars with the Philistines. They are now recognised as Egyptian in origin, adopted by Egyptian mercenaries from various ethnic and linguistic groups, including Philistines, for burial in Palestine from the thirteenth through into the twelfth century BC, and occasionally later, even as far east as Jordan.

ite population in this region from the fourteenth century BC and throughout the thirteenth, has been provided by Trude Dothan's excavations since 1972 at Deir el-Balah. This was the last important way-station from Egypt on the road to Gaza. The site was first recognised through the clandestine discovery of a cemetery of distinctive anthropoid baked clay coffins richly equipped with objects: pottery; base-metal vessels and mirrors; seals, amulets and beads; gold jewellery; stone and faience vessels. They are an instructive blend of typically Egyptian, typically Canaanite, and 'Egyptianising'. In addition, there is a selection of Cypriot and Mycenaean pottery, indicating more distant commercial contacts that were virtually to cease for a time at the outset of the Iron Age.

This excavation has been responsible for disproving the supposition that anthropoid baked clay coffins, their lids made to look like human faces with a variety of headdresses, indicate the presence of Philistines or their associates. The finds at Deir el-Balah showed that such coffins stem from a native Egyptian tradition found among the poorer classes who could not afford the expensive process of mummification. Sometime in the thirteenth century BC at the latest such coffins had been adopted by Egyptian garrison troops who were not necessarily native Egyptians. It was they who carried the custom into Canaan. There they may indeed at times have been the hallmark of intrusive peoples, foes of Egypt conquered and then employed as mercenaries; but there were times and places when they might equally well have accommodated the bodies of Canaanites, Egyptians and others.

It is the emergence of the Philistines that distinguishes the short period from about 1200 to 1150 BC in western Canaan. Although they remain one of the most widely known people mentioned in the Old Testament, their emergence in Canaan is only partially understood. They were to give their name to Palestine and were to be the most formidable opposition to the emergence of the tribes of Israel as a political force.

Ever since the earliest days in the modern study of Egyptian inscriptions in the nineteenth century, the people known as *prst* (*Peleset*) in Ramses III's account of the great invasions from the north, which he repulsed from Egypt in the eighth year of his reign (*c.* 1186/5 BC), have been identified with the *pelishti* of the Old Testament, rendered as 'Philistines' in English. In the reliefs and inscriptions carved on temple walls at Medinet Habu in Egypt that record this triumph, the *Peleset* appear (as always) in the company of other invaders. They are only once linked, in another inscription of Ramses III, to the sea, though all these invaders are commonly, if somewhat misleadingly, known in modern scholarship as 'the Peoples of the Sea'. Some of those listed in Egyptian inscriptions had been threatening Egypt and the Levant for over one hundred and fifty years. Subsequent to the victory of Ramses III, *Peleset* are listed, again among others, as garrison forces and soldiers in his service, but it is not specifically recorded that this was in Canaan.

The Old Testament refers only to Philistines, not to any of the other peoples associated with them in Egyptian records. However, the following account assumes that what applies to Philistines in Canaan may hold true for other groups of 'Sea Peoples' as well, since this accords better with the Egyptian textual evidence and the distribution of the relevant archaeological information. In the Bible the territorial power of the Philistines, once established, is seen to be in the coastal plain or in the foothills of the Shephelah. Five main cities are mentioned at Ashkelon, Ashdod, Gath, Gaza and Ekron, with some reference to at least two minor ones, at Timnah and Ziklag. According to Old Testament sources, which date from hundreds of years after the first Philistines reached Canaan, they came ultimately from 'Caphtor' (*Amos* 9:7; *Jeremiah* 47:4). Modern scholars have usually associated this region with the Egyptian term 'Keftiu' and the 'Kaptara' of cuneiform sources from Mari and Ugarit; all are taken to denote Crete or possibly the Aegean region in general. This Biblical idea of an Aegean origin for the Philistines has played an important role in modern study of them.

Although controversy still surrounds the identification of some of the primary Philistine settlements mentioned in the Old Testament, a broad measure of agreement has followed recent excavations. Ashdod, whose location is not disputed, was excavated by the Dothans between 1962 and 1972 and the results of this work are fundamental to Trude Dothan's major

32 Drawing of a relief at Medinet Habu in Egypt, showing part of the battle between the Egyptian pharaoh Ramses III (*c.* 1194–1163 BC) and the so-called 'Sea Peoples', including Philistines. The invaders are distinguished by the splayed or 'feather' head-dress (its exact nature is unknown) and their use of heavy, ox-drawn carts with solid wheels, as well as spoke-wheeled, light war-chariots drawn by horses.

study, *The Philistines and their Material Culture* (Jerusalem 1981). This is one of the very rare works of synthesis in the archaeology of Palestine accessible to the layman. Tell esh-Sharia, probably ancient Ziklag, was excavated by Eliezer Oren from 1972 to 1978. Major excavations are currently proceeding at Ashkelon, under Stager's direction, at Tel Miqne (?Ekron) under Trude Dothan and Seymour Gitin, and at Tel el-Batashi (?Timnah) under Kelm and Mazar. The results may be expected in due course to increase very significantly our knowledge of the archaeology of the earliest Philistine settlements, since it remains in many respects obscure.

In the first place, the Egyptian records are at best ambiguous, at worst wholly obscure. The enigmatic text on the 'Israel Stela' of Merneptah shows that by his reign already in the later thirteenth century BC there were problems for Egyptian rule over south-west Canaan. In a historical hypothesis made popular by Albright and Alt, among others, the Philistines and other 'Sea Peoples' became a settled element in the population of Canaan when Ramses III (*c.* 1194–1163 BC), after repelling their invasion in his year 8, settled them in what was to be Philistia, as a buffer against foes of Egypt farther afield in Canaan. But it is possible that Ramses III had had to contend with intruders who had already seized parts of the Canaanite coastal plain before they attacked Egypt. Then, repulsed from the frontiers of Egypt by him, they simply established themselves more firmly in and around Gaza in city-states largely, if not completely, independent of Egyptian rule. The 'Egyptianisation' of the Philistines, as reflected in their material culture, could have arisen from commercial or intermittent military contacts as easily as from domination by Egyptians.

If the hypothesis of the settlement of Philistines through garrisons under the Egyptian aegis in the years from about 1185 to 1150 BC is abandoned in favour of the view that they were there already on their own terms, this does not directly affect interpretations of the archaeological evidence; but it requires us to look rather differently at the years of declining Egyptian rule in Canaan. Whatever precisely happened, there was some kind of *détente* between Egyptians and 'Peoples of the Sea' in south-west Canaan until about the mid-twelfth century that allowed for a marked degree of Egyptian control or interest as far afield as Megiddo, where there is textual evidence relating to pharaohs as late as Ramses VI (*c.* 1151–1143 BC).

It is this first phase of Philistine occupation in Canaan that has proved most elusive to archaeological investigation. In recent years the archaeological hallmark for the first intrusive groups of 'Sea Peoples' has been identified as a class of painted Mycenaean pottery, classified by specialists as type 'III C:lb'. This has been found in occupation levels of the first half of the twelfth century BC at Ashdod and Tel Miqne, the supposed site of ancient Ekron. Such pottery appears sporadically elsewhere in the Levant and in Cyprus. In colour, shapes and painted motifs it is faithful to the long-established Mycenaean Greek tradition of potting. Chemical and physical analyses of this pottery, from sites both in Cyprus and in Canaan, have indicated that it was made locally. Thus, it is argued, the potters not the pots were intrusive. This has suggested to many scholars that the intruders belonged to a single ethnic group whose homeland lay in the Aegean or in western Turkey. This hypothesis has been fortified by its coincidence with the Biblical idea of a western homeland, in 'Caphtor', for the Philistines.

The pottery long known as 'Philistine', from its concentration on sites in south-west Canaan linked with them in the Old Testament, appears in stratified archaeological contexts as the occurrence of Mycenaean III C:lb pottery begins to decline, probably from an advanced date in the reign of Ramses III (*c.* 1194–1163 BC) or soon thereafter. This is evident, for instance, at Ashdod and Tel Miqne, at Tell el-Farah (South) and Tell esh-Sharia, and in the settlement established at Tel Qasile about this time (see below). This pottery is a hybrid that evolved locally in Philistia. It should not, however, be assumed (as it commonly was at one time) that wherever it appears there were Philistines or their associates in occupation. Like all attractively painted pottery, it was traded and used by people of diverse ethnic origins. These potters used red and black matt paint, in contrast to the lustrous Mycenaean pottery, on some shapes that were local to Canaan and in clays that were also indigenous. However, many of the shapes and designs were inspired by Mycenaean patterns, notably a preference for birds and certain geometric forms like antithetic spirals. As there had been a local bichrome painted pottery style in Late Bronze Age Canaan, caution is still needed in assessing how much of the inspiration for the painted 'Philistine' pottery was indeed foreign. In general it illustrates exposure to a variety of cultural influences by peoples now sufficiently settled to evolve styles of their own. Physical and chemical analyses of this pottery have shown that much of it was made in the coastal area, at places like Tel Qasile, then carried inland and northwards by trade and social contact to places like Tell

33 A general view, looking west over temple 131, in stratum X of Mazar's excavations at Tel Qasile. In the foreground is the entrance to the 'Philistine' temple (from the right); beyond it, with a central column base, the main room of the shrine. Compare 34, where a second column is reconstructed on the podium.

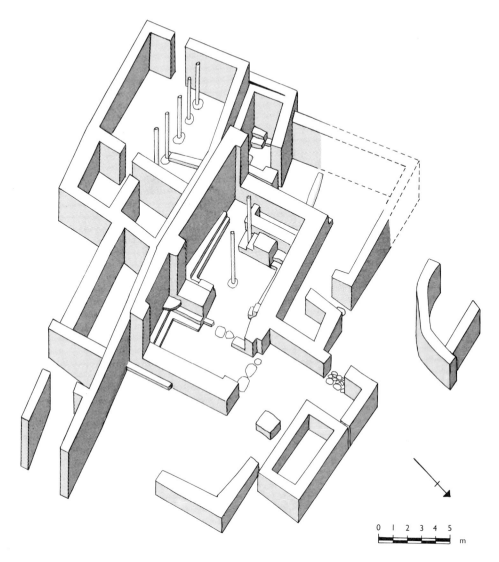

34 Isometric plan of the temple at Tel Qasile, in stratum x, looking south-west. This is a 'Philistine' settlement, and this religious complex has been attributed to them. Compare 33, showing this site in course of excavation.

Eitun near Tell Beit Mirsim, to Beth-Shan and Deir Alla, to Megiddo and Tel Dan.

It was in the second half of the twelfth century BC that the Philistines really established themselves by rebuilding older towns and founding new ones, often no doubt in close association with the Canaanite population they now ruled. Ashdod was remodelled to a new layout and strongly fortified. At Tel Qasile, in the northern suburbs of modern Tel Aviv on the Yarkon River, a new maritime settlement was established. Elsewhere there is a varied archaeological record of urban recession, as at Aphek and Lachish, or of richly equipped cemeteries, as at Azor, where the contemporary settlement remains unknown. Thriving urban developments are evident at this time farther up the coast, as at Dor where another 'Sea People', the *Tjeker*, were involved, according to Egyptian sources, or in the Plain of Acre at the recently excavated Tel Keisan. All illustrate the mixed cultural patterns of western Canaan immediately after Egypt had finally withdrawn. It was hereabouts, and northwards up the coast into modern Lebanon, that the Phoenicians were now developing the vital urban and maritime culture that was to continue Canaanite traditions most vigorously and bring them enduring fame as disseminators of the alphabet and other skills to the Greek world.

Full publication of the three 'Philistine' levels of occupation at Tel Qasile, with its wide range of pottery and other finds, has made it currently the best place to observe the newcomers as they settled down to evolve their own urban life-style. From the outset the town was focused on a relatively small shrine ('the house of the god') set within a large enclosure; in later periods, from the twelfth through into the tenth century BC, it was rebuilt on a larger scale and with variations in plan, but the orientation and the location of the 'Holy of Holies' went unchanged (34). The temples were integrated with other buildings to form a block surrounded by streets. Amihai Mazar, the excavator, has shown how these temple plans, though initially in the Canaanite tradition as represented by a temple in area C at Hazor, relate much more closely to shrines at Kition in Cyprus, at Phylakopi on the island of Melos in the Aegean, and at Mycenae in Greece.

A fascinating variety of decorated baked clay stands and cult bowls, vessels for pouring liquids, anthropomorphic and zoomorphic vessels, and masks were associated with the Tel Qasile shrines, some for use in ritual meals, some for libations. The cultural traditions represented here are as heterogeneous as those already detected in other aspects of Philistine culture. There are Canaanite and Egyptian features; strong links with Cypriot cult objects; and scattered traces of a distinctive type of baked clay female figurine, best known through finds at Ashdod (the 'Ashdoda mourning women'), whose Aegean ancestry has been generally acknowledged (36).

35 Group of pottery vessels from stratum x at Tel Qasile. It includes examples of the distinctive painted pottery, dating after *c.* 1150 BC, long associated with the Philistines (red and black on white slip); especially centre left.

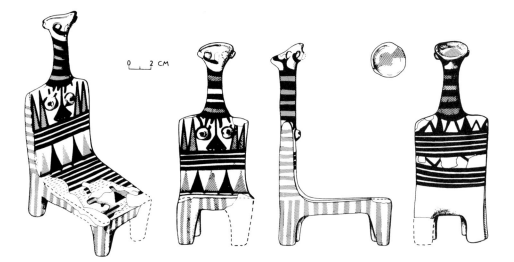

36 Drawings of a painted baked clay 'Ashdoda' female figurine, with body merging into a four-legged chair or couch, perhaps used as an offering tray. It is from the floor of a house in the twelfth-century 'Philistine' settlement at Ashdod. These figurines have been linked to Mycenaean Greek terracotta statuettes.

The physical aspects of the cult at Tel Qasile, in so far as archaeology can reveal them, do not differ from those of Bronze Age Canaanite cults. They appear to complement Biblical evidence that the Philistines worshipped gods with Semitic names (*Judges* 16:23; 1 *Samuel* 5:2). The existence of two adjacent shrines in the eleventh century is, however, only paralleled in Cyprus and the Aegean, not yet in Canaan. The eighth-century BC ostracon found on the surface at Tel Qasile with the inscription: '(G)old (of) Ophir. (Belonging) to Beth Horon/30 sh(ekels)' might be taken to mean that the god worshipped here in the earlier shrines was *Horon*, a well-known Canaanite deity mentioned in texts from Ugarit and from Egypt in the New Kingdom. The accumulation of ash, bones and sherds in the courtyard and outside the temple area has been taken as evidence for sacrifices and ritual meals. Since temples often served as town treasuries, the donation of gold to 'Beth Horon' (the 'house or temple' of Horon) would be doubly appropriate.

Soon after their discovery a quarter of a century ago it was suggested that some clay tablets from Deir Alla in the Jordan Valley, written in an enigmatic linear script which is still undeciphered, were the work of the Philistines or other 'Sea Peoples'. They were found in destruction debris that included a faience vessel bearing the cartouche of Queen Tausert as pharaoh of Egypt, true only of her last two regnal years (*c.* 1198–1196 BC). As this writing is wholly unlike any known Canaanite script of the time, but vaguely resembles the so-called 'Cypro-Minoan' writing of Cyprus in the Late Bronze Age, it does indeed seem to be intrusive. If this association is a clue to its origin, then it might possibly have something to do with one or other of the 'Sea Peoples'; but, if it does, then it belongs early in their contacts with the Canaanites.

To this phase also belongs an intensively used cemetery on the lower tell at neighbouring Tell es-Saidiyeh excavated first by an American expedition, led by Pritchard from 1964 to 1965, and currently by a British Museum team directed by Tubb. Certain aspects of the burial customs and the material equipment found in this cemetery have raised the possibility that some, if not all, of the people buried here were from the diverse groups loosely associated by modern scholarship as 'Peoples of the Sea'. At this time (*c.* 1200–1150 BC), there was a strongly fortified settlement on the main tell, with an elaborate water system. The graves contain, among other things, pottery and ivory objects of Egyptian design with an unusually wide range of forms – bowls, trays, strainers, juglets and lamps – in bronze rather than the more normal baked clay (37). Such 'drinking sets' have Egyptian precursors and are found on sites where the baked clay anthropoid coffins of Egyptian ancestry have also been excavated (31). Two bodies, moreover, found in the cemetery in 1964–5 had been crudely mummified by wrapping them in cloth and then encasing them in bitumen blocks. This practice, so far unknown earlier in Canaanite cemeteries, recalls Egyptian funerary customs just as the anthropoid coffins do. Whether these were Egyptian mercenary garrisons penetrating deep into the Jordan Valley or newcomers acting on their own initiative about 1200 BC, remains to be seen.

A famous passage in 1 *Samuel* 13:19–20 referring to the time of Saul has often been interpreted to mean that the Philistines had long enjoyed a monopoly of iron-production (though the Bible does not mention any specific metal), as well as of all metalworking: 'There was not a single smith in the whole land of Israel, because the Philistines had reasoned: We must prevent the Hebrews from forging swords or spears. Hence all the Israelites were in the habit of going down to the Philistines to sharpen every plough-share, axe, mattock or goad'. Neither is likely to be true, save possibly for a short period in the tenth century BC. Unfortunately, though iron ore is generally available in Philistia and in Canaan (cf. *Deuteronomy* 8:9), there is no unequivocal archaeological evidence yet to show that it was being smelted there in the early Iron Age, despite many claims to the contrary. Remains of furnaces and other industrial installations there are, but their

37 Bronze drinking set, including a jug, a shallow drinking bowl and a filter, from one of the very early Iron Age graves at Tell es-Saidiyeh, Jordan; recently excavated by a British Museum Expedition directed by Tubb.

role is still problematic at such sites as Tells Jemmeh, Mor and Qasile. More often than not this evidence indicates copper- or bronze- rather than iron-working. As the number of iron objects datable to the twelfth and eleventh centuries increases, they continue to indicate that even before they settled in Canaan the Philistines and their associates may have had a knowledge – unknown to local inhabitants at that time – of how to manufacture weapons and tools of iron. Only iron trinkets had been current in Palestine and Transjordan in the Late Bronze Age. This expertise gave the Philistines an initial advantage that they retained for some time. However, the relevant technological knowledge soon spread into Canaan, perhaps as iron objects were traded into Canaanite and Israelite settlements.

It is possible that in the early Iron Age metalworking in Palestine was more decentralised than it had been in the Late Bronze Age and supplies of copper and tin may have been less predictable, so that locally available iron ores and local expertise became crucially important. In such circumstances, at a time of regional differences, ethnic labels such as 'Philistine' are hardly appropriate for technological changes. The 'Peoples of the Sea' may have inspired greater manufacture of iron in Canaan, but independent socio-economic factors promoted its diffusion throughout the region, where iron objects do not become common until the tenth century BC. There is no reason to suppose early iron was superior to bronze in hardness; some was, some was not. It is likely that the availability of iron ores and the smaller amounts of charcoal consumed in iron-production were more persuasive in its gradual adoption in preference to bronze for working tools and weapons.

It is at this time that distinctive bronze objects in graves at sites like Beth-Shan, Megiddo, Deir Alla and Tell es-Saidiyeh suggest a resurgence of the Canaanite bronze industry in the Plain of Esdraelon and in the Jordan Valley, where a number of sites also offer evidence for local metalworking. This may be the background against which we should understand the fact that the master craftsman from Tyre, who came to make the bronze-work for Solomon's Temple, did the casting 'in the plain of the Jordan ... in the foundry between Succoth [perhaps Deir Alla] and Zarethan [perhaps Tell es-Saidiyeh]' (1 *Kings* 7:46–7), where presumably not only fuel, metals and materials for moulds were readily available, but also craftsmen whose families had been skilled in using them for centuries. It is significant that both at Deir Alla and at Tell es-Saidiyeh excavation has shown that for a time after the twelfth century the main mounds were uninhabited and used only for industrial activities, perhaps seasonally by craftsmen living elsewhere. More scientific study is needed of the evidence retrieved from this phase before the nature of their activity can be accurately described.

The period when the Philistines came into increasingly hostile contact with the people of Israel, from about 1100 BC, has not yet been as extensively studied by archaeologists as the earlier phase of settlement, nor is much known of their maritime activities at this time. But there is no reason to doubt that by the late eleventh century the Philistines had pressed deep into western Judah and north-central Israel, as the Old Testament indicates. They seem also to have been increasingly assimilated into the local population.

The appearance of a type of pottery known to archaeologists as Palestinian Bichrome Ware in the Lebanon, in Cyprus, at Tel Qasile in the second half of the eleventh century, in the Egyptian Delta and at Tel Masos in the northern Negev, has been taken to indicate the beginning of widespread Phoenician trade. It is likely that it was the growth of Phoenician sea-power in the tenth century, David's victories and an alliance between Egypt and the United Monarchy, that began the eclipse of Philistine authority and their retreat into the region traditionally known as Philistia by about 900 BC.

5. The eclipse of Canaan

II: The Israelites

When most people speak of the Conquest of Canaan by the people of Israel what they have in mind is the account given in *Joshua* 1–12, which suggests that the 'promised land' was conquered from the east, across the Jordan, in a single rapid military campaign with sharp thrusts to the north (Hazor) and to the south (Lachish). This is one of the most successful conceptual models ever used by a historian, since this carefully contrived pan-Israelite version of events has virtually succeeded in eliminating from the reader's mind the infinitely more complex and confused pattern of events that emerges from a closer reading of the Old Testament.

Judges 1 : 1–2, 5, for example, provides a more fragmentary account of the intrusion. It describes the military enterprises more as a matter of actions by individual tribes than as the achievement of all the tribes of Israel, and varies in its account of the extent of territory conquered. Then, scattered elsewhere through the Old Testament, there are other divergent passages that bear to a greater or lesser degree upon the entry into Canaan, but were neither assimilated into the canonical account nor fully suppressed in editing. Clearly the most formative of ancient Israel's historians used a multiplicity of sources describing a complex series of events from different points of view, some oral, some probably written in both poetry and prose. From these diverse accounts they compounded a single version.

Modern writers on the history of early Israel have been no less active in formulating hypotheses to explain the settlement of the Hebrews in Canaan, where, both ancient and modern sources are largely agreed, they were intruders. It is the date and nature of this entry, or entries, that are still debated. Diverse as the modern arguments are, they have a marked tendency to seek a single explanatory model to serve for every region and every circumstance in the extended process that gave Israel supremacy over Canaan. They have to be read very carefully to reveal the points they have in common. They are not quite as exclusive as they seem. The growing body of information retrieved through excavation and survey supports the Old Testament account by indicating that the process was extended, various and often complex. It varied from region to region, often within regions, and is not simply explained in terms of conquest, migration or internal revolt.

In the past half century three primary explanations have emerged, epitomised by the three processes just mentioned. German scholars, resting their case primarily on the internal evidence of the Old Testament text in all its diversity, have pioneered the view that the settlement was in the main a peaceful process of migration in which military conflict was secondary. Initially groups of Israelites infiltrated into sparsely occupied areas of Canaan, forming tribal units in the remote hill country and isolated valleys, only latterly coming into conflict with the Canaanite city-states.

In contrast, an influential American school of thought pioneered by Albright and supported by many Israeli scholars has largely accepted the primarily military character of the entry into Canaan. They have sought to confirm a conquest through archaeological investigation. It was Albright in particular who stressed the excavated evidence for destruction of Canaanite towns at the end of the Late Bronze Age and linked this with the Biblical account of Joshua's conquest.

More recently a third explanation has emerged, proposed by Mendenhall in 1962 and much expanded by Gottwald, notably in a massive study significantly entitled *The Tribes of Yahweh: A Sociology of the Religion of Liberated Israel, 1250–1050 B.C.E.* (1979). This is a much more speculative sociological hypothesis influenced, as Gottwald has made clear, by radical religious and political undercurrents in American thinking in the 1960s and earlier 1970s. His proposal starts with the assumption that there was a recognisable Hebrew population within Canaan at least by the Late Bronze Age. By then it was socially and politically deprived. This concept of a repressed local peasantry, fired by egalitarian principles and covenant theology to overthrow their Canaanite 'feudal' overlords, replaces more completely than any other hypothesis the traditional conception of the intrusive Israelites (or Hebrews) as a people of nomadic or semi-nomadic origin from the periphery of Canaan, who learnt the skills of farming in Canaan and then in their turn adopted an urban way-of-life.

As Albright laid such emphasis on the role of archaeology in the reconstruction of the history of the emergence of the Israelites, it is not surprising that it was his hypothesis that for so long dominated discussions of the relationship between archaeological evidence and the Old Testament text. As we noticed earlier, this was at a time when archaeological inquiry concentrated almost exclusively upon the excavation of isolated mounds, usually those of considerable size whose Biblical identity was reasonably well established, rather than on changing patterns of settlement in specific geographical zones. Famous sites first excavated in the heyday of 'Biblical archaeology', between the two World Wars, such as Ai, Hazor, Jericho and

38 General view of Et-Tell, usually identified as the site of ancient Ai, which excavations have shown was uninhabited between *c.* 2400 BC and the early or mid-eleventh century BC, when an unfortified village was established there.

Tell ed-Duweir (Lachish), were reinvestigated after 1952 with a dramatic impact on the pan-Israelite invasion hypothesis. These revisions will be briefly examined in turn, since they throw significant light on the current relationship between the Bible and archaeology in this crucial instance.

Ai (38) was first excavated from 1933 to 1935 by Judith Marquet-Krause, whose premature death brought work to a precipitate end; then again from 1964 to 1972 by Callaway. Both excavations showed that the site was not occupied between the destruction of the Early Bronze Age town about 2350 BC and the establishment of a village on the site in the early Iron Age. The newcomers then were mainly farmers attempting to secure a living in the inhospitable hills of central Canaan. Many efforts have been made to explain away the absence of evidence at Ai for Joshua's attack, but none is really satisfactory. On the whole it is probable that there is no historical foundation for this account as we have it.

Hazor, first tested by Garstang in 1928, was more fully excavated by Yadin from 1955 to 1958. The final destruction of the Canaanite city at Hazor, after which the enormous Lower City was never again inhabited, was dated by Yadin to the last quarter of the thirteenth century BC on the evidence of the relatively closely dated Mycenaean Greek pottery sherds found in the debris. Some scholars now date it prior to 1250 BC. Sometime in the twelfth century BC, after an interval of unknown length, semi-nomadic or transient peoples lived in the Upper City, on top of the old mound, in

71

39 View of Callaway's excavations in the stone-built village established on the mound at Ai in the eleventh century BC.

huts or tents, leaving traces of their simple life-style in nothing more than rough foundations, cooking installations and storage pits. These remains have subsequently been interpreted as the earliest efforts of a group of intrusive Israelites penetrating the region. A truly urban settlement was not established at Hazor again until the Solomonic period (see chapter 6). This archaeological sequence led Yadin to conclude that 'the historical source concerning the Deborah–Sisera Battle is contained in the Deborah Song (*Judges* 5) which does not mention Hazor at all, and the mention of Jabin ['the king of Canaan who reigned in Hazor'] in the prose version (*Judges* 4) must be attributed to a later editor, who tried to ascribe the historical background to the Battle of the Valley of Jezreel.'

There are few Biblical passages as well known as the account of the fall of Jericho to the invading Israelites recounted in *Joshua* 6. It was inevitable that the pioneers of archaeology in Palestine should see in it a primary test-case for the new discipline. Surely, they argued, here if anywhere was a place where excavation would reveal the city wall that had 'collapsed then

40 A view of Kathleen Kenyon's excavations at Jericho, showing one of the few vestiges of Late Bronze Age settlement found on the eroded surface of the mound. In the centre are the foundations of a Late Bronze Age house; to the left, a small area of the contemporary floor.

and there' at 'the sound of the trumpet'. In his excavations (1930–6) at Tell es-Sultan, universally accepted as the site of ancient Jericho since early Christian times, Professor Garstang uncovered the remains of a stage in the town wall that had apparently collapsed in this manner, with, against it, evidence of a terrific conflagration. It was ascribed by Garstang to the time of Joshua and rapidly became the key illustration in any attempt to demonstrate the role of archaeology in proving the 'truth' of the Biblical text. A generation later, in Kathleen Kenyon's excavations at Jericho from 1952 to 1958, it was demonstrated that the wall in question was the final phase of the wall that had surrounded the Early Bronze Age town about 2350 BC. More to the point, the renewed excavations showed that the top of the mound at Jericho had suffered massive depletion by erosion, leaving very few traces of occupation above the Middle Bronze Age defences. Even they were denuded. They could have survived sufficiently to be repaired for use in the Late Bronze Age, but since so much had disappeared, it is likely that nothing at all of the walls of the later town, of the period to which the entry into Canaan is commonly attributed, has survived. Even if the whole of the top of Tell es-Sultan were to be excavated, it is unlikely that this would provide any evidence for the defences of the Late Bronze Age town.

Excavations have, however, produced enough evidence to show that there was a Late Bronze Age settlement at Jericho and to give some slight evidence of the date at which it was destroyed. Over nearly the whole excavated area the houses of the Middle Bronze Age, and anything later, had shared the fate of the defences and had disappeared through erosion. One small area of the Middle Bronze Age town survived on the east side, adjacent to the spring. The houses had been destroyed by fire at the end of the Middle Bronze Age, in the first half of the sixteenth century BC. Afterwards there was an abandonment during which erosion carried the burnt debris down the slope of the mound, to create a thick layer over the earlier seventeenth-

41 Aerial view of the mound at Tell ed-Duweir (Lachish), with the areas opened up by the current Israeli excavations directed by Ussishkin. In the centre is the palace–fortress of the time of the Divided Monarchy; to the lower right are the excavations in and around an important fortified city gate, whence came the inscribed bronze fragment shown in 42. On the far right is the Assyrian siege mound before recent excavation (see 84).

to sixteenth-century houses. Overlying this debris layer there survived at the east end of the excavated area the stone foundations of a single wall. This wall was so close to the modern surface that only about a square metre of the contemporary floor survived; elsewhere the modern surface cut down into it. The one juglet surviving on its surface, lying by a small clay oven, and a limited amount of Late Bronze Age pottery beneath the floor, suggest that the building is late fourteenth century in date. Garstang had found a much damaged clay tablet inscribed in cuneiform script that may also be fourteenth century in date.

The best evidence for dating the reoccupation of the site after this period of abandonment comes from the tombs excavated during the 1930–6 excavations. Professor Garstang was misled in the interpretation of the evidence from them by misdatings of sixteenth- to fourteenth-century pottery, current at that time. He also failed to realise that in these rock-cut tombs the latest burial is usually at a low level in the front of the tomb, with the remains of earlier burials pushed back and mounded up at the rear. Absolute height of burials within the tomb chamber means nothing and Professor Garstang was led to believe that later objects found on the same level as earlier ones were contemporary. A wholly false impression of continuity and early chronology was thus given. The finds in the tombs cleared in Kenyon's excavations indicated that a very few of the Middle Bronze Age tombs were reopened and some later burials were placed in them. Associated with the burials in this period of Late Bronze Age reuse were Mycenaean Greek vessels, which probably belong to the second half of the fourteenth century BC. Thus there was settlement on the tell from about 1400 to 1325 BC, or even for a generation or so longer. Thereafter the earliest evidence for renewed settlement is isolated pottery vessels dating from the eleventh into the tenth century BC.

In summing up the results of the Wellcome–Marston Expedition's excavations at Tell ed-Duweir (Lachish) from 1932 to 1938, Miss Tufnell concluded in 1958 that two dates were possible for the destruction of the final Bronze Age town: 'that of Merenptah's raid ... and one just before Rameses III's defeat of the invading northerners. There are substantial arguments in favour of each of these dates, and within this very narrow margin it is unlikely that the matter will be solved.' As so often in archaeology, even the most judicious of statements, and this is unusually so, may soon be confounded by events. When Professor Ussishkin renewed excavations at Lachish in 1973 establishing the correct date for this destruction was one of his main objectives. He was to be unusually lucky in this respect. In 1978 a deep probe into destruction levels of the last major Canaanite town at the site of a city gate revealed a cast-bronze fragment bearing the name of the Egyptian pharaoh Ramses III in a cache of bronze

42 Substantial bronze fragment with rivet holes, from some kind of public monument, or possibly the city gates, at Lachish, giving part of the name of the Egyptian pharaoh Ramses III (*c.* 1194–1163) BC). It is written in hieroglyphs within the horizontal bracket (or *cartouche*) that distinguishes royal names in Egyptian inscriptions.

objects sealed by destruction debris (42). Thus the destruction could not have occurred before the accession of Ramses III to the throne of Egypt. This pharaoh is now dated approximately to the period 1194–1163 BC. Such a substantial bronze fitting, likely to be from an architectural setting, even if allowed a minimum life, makes it likely that Canaanite Lachish was devastated sometime in the second quarter of the twelfth century BC. This is well over a generation later than many scholars had previously supposed.

By the end of the 1970s it was apparent, in the light of excavation on an increasing number of tells, that the eclipse of Canaan had been a protracted and complex process, varying from area to area, as indeed a careful reading of the Old Testament suggests. Where destructions were evident in towns they differed significantly in date and were therefore most unlikely to have been the result of one and the same military offensive from east of the Jordan. At all sites where there were positive signs of sharp breaks in occupation the agents of change were anonymous; no victory stelae bore witness to their identity, no aspect of material culture was unequivocally diagnostic of their ethnic origin. The archaeological evidence indicated, moreover, that many of the Canaanite cities said to have been conquered by Joshua were not in existence at the end of the Late Bronze Age, conspicuous amongst them Ai, Arad, Heshbon and Jericho, whilst others, like Dan and Gibeon (el-Jib) had such meagre remains of this period as to be 'villages' rather than 'towns'. Nor was there any major change in material culture. Were it not for the Old Testament, no invasion would have been suspected at this time.

It was at this point that the results of surface surveys in carefully selected areas began to produce more positive results. The way had been pointed over thirty years ago by Aharoni in his study of Upper Galilee. Though his conclusions have been modified by more recent work (and the area is in some respects now seen to be unusual), they stimulated a whole generation of local archaeologists to pursue comparable surface surveys in similar well-defined geographical zones. There has been a marked concentration of such studies in the hill country of modern Israel, in the two regions of the tribes of Ephraim and Manasseh, which had an important place in the penetration of Canaan by the peoples of Israel according to Biblical tradition. Here surveys have shown that there was a marked recession in rural settlement during the Late Bronze Age, followed in the twelfth century by a proliferation of unwalled villages. The contrast with Judah to the south is marked. There relatively few new sites are found in the early Iron Age in the Judean Hills and in Benjamin, though neither had been much occupied in the Late Bronze Age and they were presumably equally open to intruders. In the early Iron Age Ephraim and Manasseh have nine or ten times the number of new settlements. It is interesting to notice that in Manasseh, which has a generally favourable environment for agriculture, a significant Canaanite population also flourished into the Iron Age. In the much less hospitable and almost empty landscape of Ephraim the newcomers formed a more homogeneous group, with Shiloh as the focus of their settlements.

In the primary stage of occupation the new settlers were cereal farmers and pastoralists. Wherever possible they exploited the available farming land by terracing, if necessary, and by managing whatever water supplies were available through cisterns and simple irrigation techniques. Plastered water cisterns were once regarded as diagnostic of the pioneering Israelite settlers in Galilee and elsewhere, but it is now known that they had appeared earlier in Canaan and were only used sporadically on early Israelite sites. Iron tools increasingly facilitated agricultural work in the recently exploited areas for the necessary clearance of forests and the basic tasks of other rural craftsmen. As time went on these farmers turned more and more to the cultivation of the grape and the olive.

The earliest 'Israelite' settlements vary in size and layout, but they generally conform to a pattern that is different from the towns and villages so far investigated in Late Bronze Age Canaan. Examples of these new villages, to cite but a few, have now been excavated at Dan in the north, at Ai, at Izbat Sartah and at Shiloh in the hill country north of Jerusalem, at Giloh in the south, and at various places in the Negev. Defences appear to have been minimal, save where a fort was clearly intended. Houses were often arranged in an outer ring, as if to provide their own defensive cordon, with large open spaces within the settlement. These would have accommodated flocks when necessary and provided room for storage pits. Some scholars have seen in this arrangement of living accommodation a direct descent from tented camps.

Within the villages themselves the typical unit seems to have been the family compound. The stone-built houses are usually made up of three or four rooms in which stone pillars played an important structural role. It has been assumed that the pillared areas remained partly unroofed; but when only foundations survive such conclusions have always to be tentative. There may, on occasions, have been roofs and upper storeys. It was for long thought that this type of house only appeared in Canaan with the arrival of newcomers in the twelfth century BC, but there are now some indications that it had ancestors in Canaan in rural areas which have only recently become the subject of careful archaeological study. Certainly this house type came to be widely distributed, from Transjordan to Philistia and northwards along the coastal plain to Megiddo.

The new patterns of settlement that are now evident in the twelfth and eleventh centuries BC conform broadly to those given by a careful reading of the Old Testament accounts of the Israelite entry into Canaan. They are concentrated in the core area of Ephraim and Manasseh from the earlier twelfth century, if not before, with a population then expanding southwards into the Judean Hills and northwards into Galilee during the twelfth century, at a time when the urban heart of Canaan lay elsewhere. The early settlement of Judah was concentrated in the centre, with penetration from the later twelfth century into peripheral regions, such as the Arad–Beersheva basin. Even within the core areas of settlement the process varied, with some villages, as with that at Izbat Sartah, established in the heart of settled Canaan.

Some features of these new settlements, such as the three- or four-roomed, pillared stone houses, or storage jars with a rim like a collar (29), have been taken as markers of specifically 'Israelite' settlements. Sometimes they are, sometimes they are not; each case has to be judged individually. Social and economic, as well as ethnic factors, are closely involved in their distribution. They may not be used simplistically to map the distribution of the early

43 Aerial view of the early Iron Age village at Tel Masos with areas excavated under the direction of Fritz and Kempinski. House plans are evident on the left and on the extreme right may be seen a partially reconstructed set of pillars within a house (cf. 44).

settlements of the tribes of Israel in Canaan, since they were never used exclusively by them.

It is now established that during the Late Bronze Age Transjordan was not largely inhabited by semi-nomadic peoples, as had long been assumed on the basis of inadequate archaeological information. The recent rapid development of archaeological research in Jordan has provided evidence to suggest that there was an urban culture there not unlike that of Canaan. Then again, new and in many ways still inadequate data from surveys and isolated small excavations indicates that in the early Iron Age the small villages of Transjordan were in many respects similar to those in the highlands west of the River Jordan. Glueck argued long ago, as the result of his own pioneering field surveys, that these were the earliest settlements of the emergent Ammonites, Edomites, Israelites and Moabites in the region. Current research appears to endorse this conclusion, though reliable separation of these peoples, and probably others still undocumented, through material remains is as elusive as ever.

The problem of identity is by no means confined to Transjordan. For example, a fortress of the eleventh century high in the mountains of Upper

Galilee at Har Adir, excavated by Davis, seems to be foreign to the many local sites with the same material culture long identified as 'Israelite' unfortified villages. Is this a fort on the borders of the kingdom of Tyre built to resist further penetration by the newcomers or did the Israelites build it to defend their own growing settlements against threats from Tyre?

At the opposite end of the country – in the Negev – there is little or no evidence of settlement in the Late Bronze Age. Resettlement appears to have begun in the early Iron Age at sites like Arad, Beersheba, Tel Esdar and Tel Masos. Fritz and Kempinski, the excavators, have interpreted the relatively large unfortified village settlement of Tel Masos in the northern Negev as an outstanding example of an early Israelite settlement, whilst others, noting its exceptional buildings and small finds, prefer to attribute it to a local people like the Amalekites. The lowest level at Tel Masos, representing the earliest settlement there, consists only of beaten earth floors and pits. It has been taken to represent the home of a people in transition from nomadic to settled life in the later thirteenth century BC. In the next phase of occupation the first stone-built houses appear, with a courtyard divided by pillars and a broad room at the rear. By the next phase the four-roomed house that was to be standard in the area during the twelfth and

44 Detail of one of the village houses at Tel Masos with a set of partially restored stone pillars.

45 Bronze statuette of a humped bull found by chance near the western wall of a very early Iron Age (*c.* 1200–1100 BC) cult place on the summit of a ridge in the northern part of the Samarian hills. The bull might symbolise male divinity or refer to a specific god, as was the case in Canaan with the West Semitic storm god Hadad (Baal). In the cult of the 'golden calf' (better perhaps 'bull') in the Old Testament the animal has been variously interpreted by modern scholars either as a pedestal for Yahweh (as with the cherubim in the 'Holy of Holies' in Solomon's Temple) or as the symbol of the god of Israel or some other, perhaps foreign or Canaanite, god.

eleventh centuries is preferred. Other buildings have more marked affinities with the earlier architectural traditions of both Canaan and Egypt, suggesting a marked degree of assimilation among diverse peoples in the northern Negev in the twelfth century. Similar borrowing from the native population of southern Canaan is evident in a number of the standard types of pottery used at Tel Masos, whilst sherds of distinctively painted 'Philistine' and 'Midianite' and 'Bichrome' wares (probably from northern Canaan) indicate widely ranging contacts.

Even on the major Canaanite sites in the period of transition there are subtle and possibly revealing contrasts in the archaeological record, again highlighting clues to the very heterogeneous situation indicated in Biblical sources. At Taanach, excavated by Lapp in the 1960s, the material culture of the twelfth century settlement is very like that of the contemporary highland villages attributed to intrusive Israelites. By contrast, at Megiddo, excavated by the Americans before the Second World War, the Canaanite tradition of the Late Bronze Age persists through levels of the twelfth century.

In the earliest villages attributed to the Israelites there are none of the

46 The eastern enclosure wall, looking north, of the twelfth-century BC cult place whence came the bronze bull statuette illustrated in 45. The site was surveyed and excavated by Amihai Mazar, who thought it might be an early Israelite cult centre, perhaps a *bamah* ('high place'), though the exact nature of the cult practised here remains debatable.

public buildings commonly recognised in the towns of Canaan. It has been assumed that the open space within settlements provided accommodation for acts of public worship or political assemblies. What little archaeological evidence there is for cult sites at this early stage of settlement tends to be found away from settlements. A cult place excavated by Amihai Mazar high in the northern part of the hill country, to the north-east of Shechem, was recognised through the chance find of a bronze bull statuette (45). As the sanctuary had been set on a rocky prominence, away from settlements, erosion had removed most of the structures (46). Within a massive stone enclosure was what may have been the remains of an altar or *massebah*, possibly an open-air shrine of the *bamah* of 'high place' type. But whether this had been an 'Israelite' or 'Canaanite' cult place remains open to debate.

A rather better preserved structure has recently been excavated by Zertal on Mt Ebal. Here a sacred area (temenos) was marked out by enclosure walls. In an early phase the site was modest, focused on a round installation at its centre. Then it was reconstructed with a new temenos wall, an impressive entrance, a large rectangular altar, a terrace walk round three sides of the altar, two paved courtyards and two ramps, one onto the altar, the other giving access to the encircling terrace walk. The commonest finds were ashes, bones and pottery dated in the late thirteenth and twelfth centuries BC. The bones represented young male cattle, sheep, goat and fallow deer, which were all charred and cut off at the joints. This altar of 'burnt offering' has been interpreted as an early Israelite sanctuary.

There was, however, in stratum XI at Hazor (the level followed by structures of the Solomonic period) a cult place associated with an unwalled village. In it were baked clay incense stands. Among votive objects found in a jar was a bronze statuette of a seated male in a conical headdress, a bronze axehead, a dagger and javelin heads. As such objects are typical of Canaanite cult places, they illustrate particularly well the difficulty archaeologists face in any attempt to give ethnic labels to such material culture. This settlement was attributed by the excavator, Yadin, to the Israelites, but in view of the finds this should perhaps still be regarded as an open question.

How then do the explanatory models for the emergence of Israel in Canaan described at the beginning of this chapter appear when tested against the present archaeological evidence? It is clearly compatible with the concept of peaceful infiltration into uninhabited or sparsely inhabited regions of Late Bronze Age and early Iron Age Canaan, with a degree of military conflict. But the mute evidence of material culture is rarely so decisive, taken alone, as to spell out which is most likely in any particular case. When we have evidence for destruction, as at Hazor and Tell ed-Duweir (Lachish), it may be separated by as much as a century and may be without any indication of who the agents of destruction were. When we have indications of resettlement or new settlement, as at Ai and Tel Masos, we cannot from the archaeological data confidently name the settlers, nor may we be certain in an absolute sense that they are 'newcomers' or 'intruders'. This is particularly so when we wish to read into those terms the idea of nomadic peoples settling down for the first time.

It is even less easy to detect in the available archaeological record the traces of a social revolution, or refugees from a supposed Late Bronze Age Canaanite feudal system, as is apparently required by advocates of the 'revolt' explanation of Israel's emergence. This may simply mean that the terms in which such a hypothesis might be tested archaeologically have yet to be worked out or that it is a theory too remote even from the internal Biblical evidence to justify such an inquiry – but that is for the textual scholars to assess. Only time, and co-operative investigation, will tell. One thing alone is now certain. No one explanatory model will accommodate either the multi-layered textual traditions of the Old Testament or the variety of evidence now available through excavation and survey. Regional trends and a rich diversity of processes through the twelfth and eleventh centuries BC saw the city-states of Canaan superseded by the United Monarchy; but not until both had responded, each in their own way, to the threats of the Philistines and their associates.

6. Palestine in the time of David and Solomon

To many people it seems remarkable that David and Solomon still remain unknown outside the Old Testament or literary sources derived directly from it. No extra-Biblical inscription, either from Palestine or from a neighbouring country, has yet been found to contain a reference to them. Yet few passages in the Old Testament are as memorable as the court chronicles for their reigns. Although they may have been elaborated by later authors, most scholars accept that the historical core is authentic. No Biblical descriptions of buildings and furniture are as precise and vivid as those of Solomon's Temple and associated palaces at Jerusalem. They seem to be a later literary reworking of two types of technical documents, instructions for builders and temple inventory lists, both well-known in ancient Mesopotamia. But whereas in Mesopotamia such texts were inscribed on clay tablets, baked to preserve them, or occasionally on stone, in Israel they are most likely to have been written in ink on papyrus and then placed in the royal archives. Only in the dry climate of Egypt have such perishable documents regularly survived. In 1952 a fragment of papyrus originally written on during the middle of the seventh century BC and reused centuries later, was found in one of the Wadi Murabbaat Caves in Israel as part of the famous Dead Sea Scrolls quest (see chapter 8). It is still a unique survivor from the period of the Monarchy, though, as will be seen, the clay sealings used to secure such rolls do survive as the only clue to the existence of papyrus archives (chapter 7).

It is important to recall that modern research has indicated how, in the time of David and Solomon, the traditional major powers of the Near East – Egypt and Mesopotamia – were in recession. It was thus easier at this particular time for the states of the Levant to assert themselves. Before, as we have seen, and afterwards, as will become evident, the local great powers mercilessly exploited their smaller neighbours as they struggled for political and economic supremacy over the east Mediterranean coast and the major routes between east and west that carried highly profitable trade and facilitated military control.

At the end of the eleventh century BC the point is reached when the

47 Jerusalem from the air before the massive urban expansion of the last forty years. On the right is the Kidron Valley, to the east of Ophel ('citadel'). In the immediate foreground is the Hinnom Valley. The area between the northern end of the ridge of Ophel (upon which the Jebusite town and the 'City of David' were built) and Temple platform are filled up by massive deposits of debris. They no longer appear to offer the fine natural defences they originally did. The Temple area is marked today by the remarkable early Islamic octagonal shrine known as the 'Dome of the Rock'.

nature of the relationship between Biblical sources and archaeology in reconstructions of ancient Israelite society changes. Although the 'historical books' of the Old Testament are often closer to being a contemporary record than the Pentateuch, it still has to be remembered at every turn that they were also edited and recast later from the point-of-view of writers sharing the preoccupations and attitudes of those who experienced the Exile and its aftermath. By that late date, half a millennium after the events treated in this chapter, Israel's political independence was over and the dynasty of David had for ever passed into oblivion. At such a time reflection, for example, on David's achievements or on Solomon's wisdom and the splendours of his court, above all upon the role of Yahweh in the destiny of his chosen people, inevitably took on a special resonance, controlling how older sources were used and presented.

From the death of Solomon sometime in the 920s BC, for the first time,

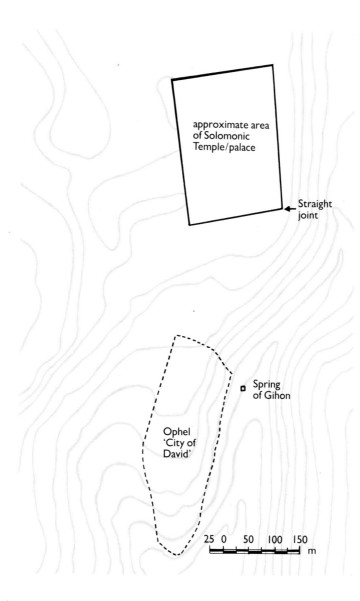

approximate area
of Solomonic
Temple/palace

Straight
joint

Spring
of Gihon

Ophel
'City of
David'

25 0   50 100 150
                    m

48 A diagram of Jerusalem in the Late Bronze and Iron Ages. Except for short
stretches of wall on the lower eastern slopes of Ophel, nothing is known for certain
of the line of the town's defensive walls at this period. It is assumed that Solomon
created a fortified 'royal quarter' in the tenth century BC for his palace and the
Temple, to the north of Ophel. But it is not yet certainly known whether this was
wholly separate from the earlier 'City of David', on the Ophel ridge to the south, or
linked to it by defensive walls. This only shows very approximately the occupied
areas in the time of the Jebusites and the United Monarchy.

49 The old city of Jerusalem seen from the east with the Temple area in the foreground. The 'Dome of the Rock' (slightly off-centre to the right), built in AD 691 by Abdul Malik, stands approximately where seventeen hundred years earlier Solomon had built a 'house' for Yahweh. The site, secured by David, might already have had a role as a cult place in earlier times when in the Bronze Age Jerusalem was a Jebusite town.

it is accepted by scholars that the Old Testament provides a dependable relative chronology, giving a framework for a historical narrative that was not available before. Despite many persisting problems over the details, the regnal years for individual rulers in Judah and Israel are now considered to be relatively certain. The margins of error in the absolute dating of their reigns are no greater than about a decade. Thus for the first time the excavator might hope to relate the occupation levels on the sites he digs with a reasonable degree of precision to an independent chronological framework. Sadly, the precision is as relative as it is variable, as a single famous example will serve to illustrate.

Samaria would appear to offer a uniquely clear point of departure for a chronological analysis of material culture, since the date of its foundation is credibly reported. In the sixth year of his reign (about 876 or 871 BC) Omri, having previously reigned at Tirzah, 'for two talents of silver ... bought a hill from Shamer and on it built a town' (1 *Kings* 16:24ff.). But the Old Testament does not say explicitly that Samaria was a virgin site, though

50 Quarrying on the southern summit of Ophel ('City of David') has removed considerable parts of the town maintained there first by the Jebusites in the Bronze Age and earlier Iron Age, then by successive rulers of Judah after David and Solomon until the Exile in the early sixth century BC.

Kathleen Kenyon, who assisted Crowfoot in his excavations there in the 1930s, assumed that it did. Consequently, she argued that the earliest pottery found at Samaria dated to Omri's reign. Israeli and American ceramic experts, comparing this pottery with that from other sites, have argued that it is earlier, belonging to the tenth or very early ninth century BC rather than to Omri's reign, and that it may have been brought to Samaria at the time when Omri's masons began work there or that it is evidence of an earlier village on the hill Omri had purchased. As a consequence Iron Age pottery chronologies among experts, depending upon which view they take, are out-of-step by a generation or so.

David's reign, in the first half of the tenth century BC, was a time of conflict and state consolidation, not of extensive royal building programmes, so no monuments have yet been positively identified as Davidic. Aharoni sought to date two buildings of ashlar masonry at Megiddo, as well as city gates at Beersheba and Tel Dan, to David's reign; but his arguments have not been widely accepted. Even at Jerusalem, where it is recorded that

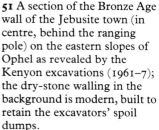

51 A section of the Bronze Age wall of the Jebusite town (in centre, behind the ranging pole) on the eastern slopes of Ophel as revealed by the Kenyon excavations (1961–7); the dry-stone walling in the background is modern, built to retain the excavators' spoil dumps.

David restored the Jebusite fortress after he had taken the city, and built a palace with the aid of craftsmen from Tyre (2 *Samuel* 5:6ff.), extensive excavations in the 'City of David' since 1961 have not yet pinpointed more than the merest traces of walls that might be Davidic. But they have clarified knowledge of the Jebusite town he captured, reputedly by a stratagem.

The original Jebusite settlement lay on the eastern ridge, south of the great Temple platform erected in later times, running down to the Pool of Siloam. The position of this town appears to have been dictated by the water supply. The only perennial spring hereabouts was the Spring Gihon, the Virgin's Fountain, in the Kidron Valley at the foot of the eastern ridge. This would have been far outside the Bronze Age city walls if they had run, as earlier excavators had supposed, close to the crest of the ridge. Access to vital water supplies from within a walled town through rock-cut shafts or galleries is a well-established feature of Palestinian town-planning; but individual examples are often difficult to date. Such a shaft and gallery exists at Jerusalem, but its head lies well down the eastern slope.

The location of the Jebusite city wall on the east was the first problem to be tackled by the Kenyon excavations (1961–7). She cut a major trench down the slope from the crest starting from walls of uncertain date exposed

52 Stepped stone structure close to the eastern crest of Ophel above the Gihon spring. Shiloh has interpreted this ramp as a reinforcement of the original Jebusite citadel, erected after David's capture of the town in the tenth century BC. It was to support David's new citadel (cf. 67).

by previous excavators in 1923–5 (51). The original town wall was found to run 48 m from the crest, well down the slope. It dated to the Middle Bronze Age in the eighteenth century BC, had been repaired under the United Monarchy and then continued in use into the eighth century BC. It was situated so as to offer good protection to the rock-cut shaft to the spring, and near enough to the latter to prevent enemy interference with the (presumably) blocked-up entrance to the spring, but not so low in the Kidron Valley as to bring it within the range of projectiles from the opposite slope.

Towards the crest of the slope first Kenyon's and then, more extensively since 1978, Shiloh's excavations have revealed an impressive structure of supporting walls and fills as the podium for the citadel of the Jebusite town, an acropolis that was to serve the same function through much of the Iron Age. Today, at this point, the visitor sees a consolidated stepped stone structure that has long been one of the most impressive vestiges of the ancient city of Jerusalem, though its date was uncertain. Shiloh has con-cluded that in the tenth century, after David had captured the city, this stepped stone structure was built as a huge supporting wall to retain the slope at this point. It overlay the remains of the earlier Jebusite citadel and served as the substructure for a new fortress: the 'Ophel' (or citadel) after which the eastern ridge is often named.

Almost nothing of the 'Citadel of David' (cf. 1 *Kings* 9:24) set on the podium dated to his time by Shiloh has yet been revealed by excavation; it may all have perished long ago to make way for subsequent buildings. The Kenyon excavations uncovered a segment of a casemate wall and a distinctive single palmette or 'Proto-Aeolic' stone capital at the northern end of the early Israelite city, but they are probably from Solomonic or post-Solomonic structures.

What the Old Testament means by the 'Millo' in reference to the building activities of David and Solomon hereabouts is uncertain. It may, as Kathleen Kenyon believed, refer to the creation of the podium for the citadel and related structures that served to level and extend the rocky surface towards the summit of the eastern ridge. Shiloh, and others, take it to mean the built-up fill across the saddle between the 'City of David' and the Temple platform. Indeed, Mazar has even identified a large Iron Age structure that he uncovered at the south-eastern corner of the Temple Mount as the 'Beth-millo' (2 *Kings* 12:20), where rebellious officers struck down King Jehoash (*c.* 835–796 BC).

In Shiloh's assessment the oldest known element in the 'City of David's' water system, long known as Warren's Shaft after its original explorer, should be dated to the later tenth or ninth century BC, after David's reign. It connected the northern part of the city, including the citadel, to its water supply. At the period to which Shiloh attributes it a number of other royal cities, such as Hazor and Megiddo, were similarly equipped with secure water systems. However, the earliest phase of such rock-cut systems is often extremely hard to date archaeologically. So late a dating for the Jerusalem water system presents problems. It is arguable that the story of David's capture of Jebusite Jerusalem, with the help of volunteers penetrating its defences up a water conduit, is a misinterpretation of a corrupt passage in the text, or indeed may refer to something other than to 'Warren's Shaft'. But still it would be surprising if the Jebusite city did not have a secure water system for times of siege. Resolving this issue is one of many problems in the archaeology of Jerusalem still to be undertaken.

Stratum 14 in Shiloh's Ophel excavations, attributed to the time of David and Solomon, yielded two significant finds for the study of cults. One was a detached bronze fist originally clenched round something now lost. It had once been part of a deity statuette standing nearly 40 cm high, which is about twice the average for known figures of this kind. The second was a fragment from a tower-shaped cult stand of baked clay decorated with the upper part of a bearded man in relief, perhaps originally carrying a kid or lamb on his shoulders. Such stands will be discussed in more detail below.

In discussing these finds we have almost certainly already passed from the reign of David into that of Solomon, whose name is forever memorably associated with Jerusalem, though little or nothing of what he built there may be confidently identified in the present archaeological record. Solomon's Temple and the associated royal palace complex had to be outside the Jebusite city on the eastern ridge, which had been repaired and refortified by David, since the structures Solomon planned were on a scale that would have required almost the whole built-up area. Expansion to the north was not difficult, for there the eastern ridge runs back towards the main line of hills without any real break. There were, nevertheless, considerable physical problems. The summit of the ridge was narrow. The provision of any large level area required the construction of an artificial platform supported by powerful retaining walls. The walls visible today at the south-east corner of the Herodian Temple platform rest on the steep rock slopes of the Kidron Valley at a depth of some 50 m below the ground level of the courtyard inside them. One can now say that, at least at this point, the substructures of Solomon's Temple courtyard must have been almost equally massive.

It is possible to make this deduction, since the position of the south-east corner of Solomon's platform can now be identified with some degree of confidence. We know from the account of the first-century AD Jewish historian Flavius Josephus (see chapter 9) that Herod the Great doubled the size of the Temple platform in his great rebuilding of the first century BC. Herod's characteristic masonry is visible in the external south and west faces of the platform. On the east side it ends abruptly against an earlier structure of entirely different masonry (95). Kathleen Kenyon, who first published this straight joint, argued that the earlier work must have belonged to the Second Temple Period and compared its style of stone-cutting to work of the Persian period at Byblos and Eshmoun, near Sidon, in the Lebanon. The restoration of Jerusalem by the returned exiles at the end of the sixth century BC, according to the Old Testament, made much use of surviving fragments of the earlier buildings, as is entirely natural. It is highly probable that considerable portions of the great platform on which Solomon's Temple stood were still visible, and much the easiest way to restore the Temple would have been to reuse the surviving foundations. Almost certainly, therefore, this straight joint gives us the position of the south-east corner of Solomon's Temple platform. No comparable straight joint is visible on the west side of the platform, where the Solomonic wall lies inside the Herodian platform. It is likely that the Solomonic structures

93

were confined to the eastern ridge, as was the rest of the early city of Jerusalem.

The Solomonic Temple thus lay some 232 metres to the north of the northern limits of the earlier 'City of David'. It seems likely that it was joined to it by a narrow strip on the summit of the ridge; but this has not yet been conclusively demonstrated by excavation and the Old Testament does not make it clear. The extension would have provided the space required by Solomon for his palaces and administrative buildings: 'As regards his palace, Solomon spent thirteen years on it before the building was completed. He built the Hall of the Forest of Lebanon ... the Hall of Pillars ... the Hall of the Throne ... His own living quarters ... And there was a house similar to this Hall for the daughter of Pharaoh whom he had taken in marriage' (1 *Kings* 7:1ff.). All the excavations since 1961 have produced only evidence of quarrying in the crucial intermediate area, undertaken from Herodian to Byzantine times, and no clear evidence for earlier structures. So it is still possible to envisage Solomon's palace and Temple as a self-contained acropolis to the north of the Davidic city.

It is unfortunate that archaeology in the Lebanon has been no more enlightening about the city and people whence the Old Testament makes clear Solomon received help and inspiration for his creation of a royal palace and temple complex in Jerusalem. At Tyre archaeology has been restrained by continuous occupation from antiquity into modern times. When systematic excavation is possible, and in that strife-ridden country it has not been in recent years, it is only in small deep soundings that do little more than offer a pottery sequence. Consequently, Solomon's buildings, more fully described in the Old Testament than any others (and reliably when it can be checked), have been reconstructed in modern times by judicious use of evidence yielded by other excavations in Syro-Palestine. This line of inquiry has been pursued continuously over the last few decades.

With an ingenious argument Ussishkin has sought to elucidate the plan of Solomon's palace. He assumes, as do a number of other commentators, that at least four of the five units listed in the Biblical text (cited above) were incorporated into one single structure. But, significantly, he then also assumes that this list takes the units consecutively (as does the Temple description), beginning at the entrance and working to the far side, as would anyone passing through the whole building from the 'hall of columns' (or portico) into the 'hall for the throne' (the king's formal place of judgement) and only thence into 'the other court': the inner area of the palace round which were grouped the domestic apartments. In seeking a contemporary model that fits this pattern Ussishkin identifies it with a type of palace, known as *bit-hiláni*, built by rulers in northern Syria and southern Turkey in the Iron Age. The 'Hall of the Forest of Lebanon' is more of an enigma

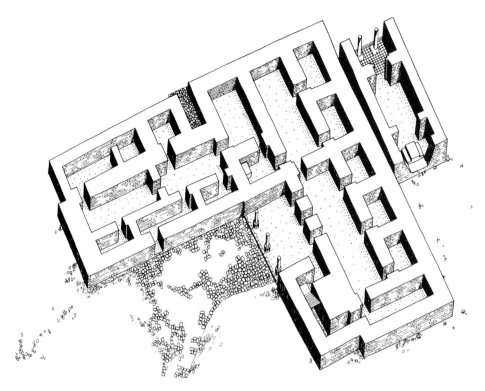

53 Isometric view of the eighth-century palace and adjacent temple in the 'second building period' at Tell Tayinat in the Amuq region of south-east Turkey. Although later than Solomon's palace and Temple in Jerusalem, this excavation (from 1935 to 1938, but only published in detail in 1971) is often cited as the best parallel to his close association of palace and temple, which was more like a 'royal chapel', immediately adjacent to the palace and on a comparatively small scale. The temple (upper right), like Solomon's, is divided internally into three areas.

and may have been a self-sufficient reception hall to one side of the palace or temple, reminiscent of multi-columned halls in the palaces of Urartu (ancient Armenia) and later in those of the great Persian kings at Persepolis in Iran.

Little new material has recently been brought to bear upon the question of the Temple's plan and furnishings. Its reconstruction still rests largely on comparisons with the ground plans of earlier Canaanite temples, such as those at Hazor, which its tripartite internal division closely resembles. To the Late Bronze Age belongs a temple complex at Kamid el-Loz in the Lebanon, excavated in the past fifteen years by a German expedition. Not only its fittings, notably the bases for two free-standing columns and an altar in front of the shrine, but also some terracotta model shrines found in the temple area recall important aspects of Solomon's Temple and again

Left **54** Carved ivory inlay, from a piece of wooden furniture, in the Phoenician style. It was found in an Assyrian royal palace at Nimrud in northern Iraq, where it probably arrived in the eighth or seventh century BC as booty or tribute. It is possible that such hybrid Egyptianising creatures as this, part human, part beast, are what is meant by the word 'cherubim' in Solomon's Temple. Tyre, whence many of the craftsmen came to work for Solomon on the Temple, was a major Phoenician craft centre.

Right **55** Carved ivory fragment from a piece of wooden furniture, found at Nimrud in Iraq, like that shown in 54. The carver has again used motifs borrowed from Egypt, as Phoenician craftsmen so often did. The men here carry jugs of a distinctive shape found in Phoenicia in metal and other materials. The Old Testament account of the decoration of Solomon's Temple suggests the use of Egyptianising themes passed on through Phoenician craftsmen.

emphasise its debt to the Canaanite tradition. An Iron Age temple at Tell Tayinat in the Antioch Valley of modern south-east Turkey, excavated in the 1930s, built some generations after Solomon's reign adjacent to a royal palace, remains the best architectural parallel for Solomon's Temple (53). The Iron Age shrine at Arad, dated by some scholars as early as the United Monarchy, is of a different, if superficially similar, architectural design owing more than Solomon's Temple did to ordinary house plans.

The minor arts of Phoenicia, notably carved ivory plaques of the eighth and seventh centuries BC, recovered in excavations at Nimrud in Assyria during excavations by Professor Mallowan and his colleagues from 1949 to 1962, still offer the best surviving clues to the carved wood decoration of the Temple's interior. The style is 'Egyptianising', as were the carved ivories of Canaan and those found long ago at Samaria, perhaps from Ahab's palace. The Biblical descriptions of the furniture of the Temple, much of it made in gold and bronze, indicate that it was also in the Canaanite metalworking tradition as known from sites like Megiddo and Tell es-Saidiyeh in the Jordan Valley, and from the related craft traditions of Cyprus, whence come the best parallels for the mobile vessel-stands made for Solomon's Temple.

The existence of minor cult places throughout the United Kingdom that kept alive many of the older forms of worship has been evident since a tenth-century building near the city gate at Megiddo yielded a group of cult objects during the American excavations there in the 1930s. These included two horned altars of limestone, cult stands of stone and baked clay, pottery chalices and other plain vessels. Lapp excavated what he believed to be a comparable cult place at Taanach in 1963, but the identification has been challenged and is certainly questionable. However, Taanach has yielded two of the most impressive known examples of a very distinctive type of cult furniture commonly dated to the tenth century. First in 1902 and then again in 1968 excavators there found two spectacular baked clay cylindrical stands, each rather like a tall tower with applied and incised decoration incorporating animals and floral motifs, monsters and nude female figures. The interpretation of this iconography is controversial, but the stands are commonly linked to the cult of the Canaanite mother-goddess Asherah. More recently, during the 1984 excavations at Pella in Jordan, Potts and the Australian team found two such tower-like baked clay cult stands, one with incised trees, the other one with two nude female figures each set above the head of a lion, as if standing on its back (56). This is, again, reminiscent of the imagery of fertility goddesses in the Bronze Age in Canaan.

One passage in particular in the Old Testament's account of Solomon's reign has long attracted the attention of archaeologists: 'This is an account of the forced labour King Solomon levied for the building of the Temple of Yahweh, his own palace, the 'Millo' and the wall of Jerusalem, Hazor,

56 Restored baked clay cult stand found in the Australian excavations at Pella in Jordan in 1984; one of the projecting heads is a restoration. It is not clear whether the surviving original is male or female. There are traces of burning in the tray, so this may indeed have been an incense-burner, as comparable objects are popularly called. The nude females set on lion heads may indicate an association with one of the Canaanite fertility goddesses.

Megiddo, Gezer ... Lower Beth-Horon, Baalath, Tamar in the wilderness, inside the country, all the garrison towns owned by Solomon, all the towns for his chariots and horses...' (1 *Kings* 9:15ff.).

Gezer, Hazor and Megiddo have become popularly known as 'Solomon's Royal Cities'. They were strategically sited to command important areas and routes throughout the kingdom. Hazor lay in the Jordan Valley, in the rich country between the Sea of Galilee and Lake Huleh, on the route to Damascus. Megiddo commanded the rich and fertile Plain of Esdraelon and, equally important, the pass over the neck of the Carmel range which was the most convenient route from Egypt to north Syria. Gezer, destroyed by an unnamed pharaoh and given as his daughter's dowry on her marriage to Solomon, lay at the foot of the hill country commanding the same route as it passed along the coastal plain. It also controlled an important road from Jerusalem down to the coast. All had been powerful Canaanite city-states, but had, for one reason or another, passed into a recession. Solomon virtually refounded them.

The buildings at Hazor attributed to Solomon's reign indicate its return to urban status. The area covered is small, consisting only of the western half of the original Upper City on the main mound, but the layout was

57 Aerial view of the multi-chambered gate (right foreground) at Hazor attributed to Solomon's masons (cf. 58). A casemate wall may be seen running up to it on the left side; just inside the wall is a pillared building of a type characteristic of Iron Age architecture. Such structures were used for various purposes, sometimes for storage as here; sometimes perhaps for stabling horses, as has been argued for a comparable building at Megiddo.

58 Detail of the fine masonry in the gate at Gezer as first revealed in Macalister's excavations there from 1902 to 1909, when it was mistakenly identified as part of a 'Maccabean Castle'.

imposing. The chief feature was a defensive casemate wall, a form of double wall linked by cross walls, which enclosed the western end of the mound and cut this off from the eastern end by a line crossing the centre. In the centre of this wall was an elaborate gateway with external towers and an entrance through a chambered gatehouse. Only the foundations of the gateway and of most of the casemate wall had survived, but there is no doubt that they form part of an elaborate and well-planned layout (57). The associated pottery showed that this layout could be dated to the mid-tenth century BC, and it was therefore reasonably attributed by Yadin to the builders of Solomon. Not much of the contemporary building within the town has been excavated, and there is no evidence that the imposing public buildings of the ninth century had Solomonic predecessors. One may, however, suppose that Solomon maintained a garrison in such a well-fortified town, and the one building excavated in detail may perhaps be identified as a barracks.

Gezer was excavated by primitive methods between 1902 and 1909, but it was, for the time, very fully published. Among the plans included by the excavator, Macalister, was one labelled 'Maccabean Castle' in which, following his excavations at Hazor, Yadin astutely thought he could detect parts of a gateway and a casemate wall of the same plan as those he had excavated in Solomonic Hazor. The pier of the Gezer gateway, moreover, was in the fine flat-dressed ashlar masonry of the best Phoenician work (58). This identification was triumphantly confirmed by the American Hebrew Union College excavations of 1964–74 at Gezer. The gate was found to be set on an artificial terrace, constructed of debris derived from a preceding destruction (59). The small finds, primarily pottery, were tenth century in date, neatly linking up with the history of Gezer at this time as related in I *Kings* 9:16–17.

Although it has long been realised that the 'Solomonic Stables' at Megiddo, as described by the American excavators in the 1930s, were not Solomonic and possibly not stables for horses, controversy has continued to surround Solomon's buildings at this site. Continuing discussion arises primarily from brief excavations undertaken there by Yadin in 1960 seeking to test hypotheses about the nature of Solomonic defences at the towns mentioned in I *Kings* 9. Although details remain to be resolved, a general view of Solomon's works at Megiddo has now been agreed.

The stratum today known as IV B–V A clearly represents an important town

59 The entire chambered gate at Gezer as revealed by American excavations in the 1960s. It is now attributed to Solomon's masons. The drain running through the centre belongs to a secondary stage in the gate's history.

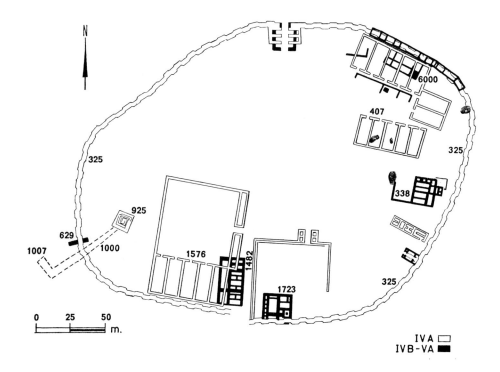

60 Plan of the major buildings at Megiddo, including those now attributed to strata
IV A; IV B–IV A (after Yadin).

dated to his reign. It has been detected all across the mound wherever levels
of occupation in the tenth century have been reached. It is separated from the
earlier, final Canaanite city by a level of simple, largely domestic structures
(stratum V B), dating to the eleventh and earlier tenth centuries. The Solomonic levels were damaged by fire, perhaps at the time of the Egyptian
invasion of Palestine under the pharaoh Sheshonq I in the reign of
Rehoboam, in the last quarter of the tenth century BC. While at Megiddo
this pharaoh erected a commemorative stela, some fragments of which were
found out of context.

In the impressive stratum IV B–V A two imposing structures ('Palaces' 1723
and 1482) were erected on the south and one (6000) on the north side of the
city, with masonry in the 'Phoenician' style. Outside them buildings, possibly store-houses, were set amid densely packed housing, which in places,
was incorporated, as were the major structures, into the defensive line round
the city; elsewhere there may have been a casemate wall at this time. Yadin
also argued that the gallery giving access to the water system was Solomonic,
though the system itself is likely to be earlier (60).

Since 1960 debate has particularly focused upon a chambered gateway at

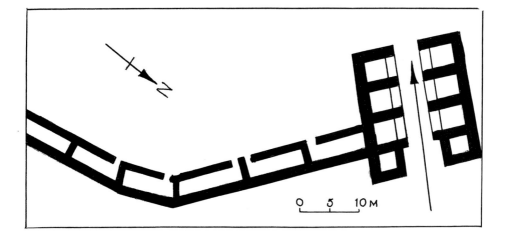

Above **61** Plan of the gate at Hazor (after Yadin).

Right **62** Plan of the chambered gate at Megiddo (after Yadin).

Below **63** Plan of the chambered gate at Gezer (after Dever; cf. 57).

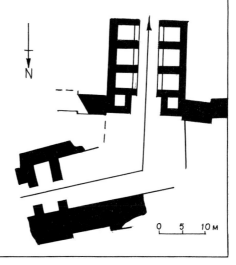

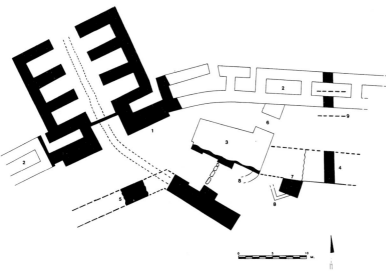

64 View of the chambered city gate attributed to Solomon's masons at Megiddo in course of excavation by an American expedition in the 1930s.

Megiddo (62), and its associated defensive wall, on account of the gate's similarity to those found at Gezer and Hazor. In 1958, when Yadin completed his Hazor excavations, only one other chambered city gatehouse of the earlier Iron Age was known: that at Megiddo. Many other city gates had been excavated but, as they were of different types, these two seemed particularly alike. But in the last twenty-five years the new excavations at Gezer already described, renewed work at Tell ed-Duweir (Lachish), where there is a comparable gate in stratum III, and the discovery of another such gate at Ashdod in 1970 increased knowledge of the size and structure of chambered gates in the tenth century BC, when they appear to have been a recurrent type. The gate at Ashdod was important in illustrating their use in Philistia, outside the kingdom of Israel. They can no longer be regarded as a type exclusively found in 'Solomon's Royal Cities'. Nor, even at that time, was there a single architectural blueprint to which Solomon's military engineers adhered rigorously. Whilst the Gezer gate is square, those at Hazor and Megiddo are rectangular, based on substructures similar in size. The examples at Ashdod and Lachish also illustrate how construction methods might be similar, but details of form and dimensions varied as best suited defensive requirements on individual sites. They may, however, both date after Solomon's reign, as that at Lachish is likely to be the work of Rehoboam's builders (cf. 2 *Chronicles* 11:9).

The 'Stables' at Megiddo are not the only case where in recent years a long association with Solomon's name has been broken. Fifty years ago when Glueck excavated the settlement of Tell el-Kheleifeh, just north of Aqabah, first discovered and identified as Solomon's Ezion-Geber by Fritz Frank, he believed that he had found evidence of copper refineries in the town. It is now known that these finds belong to a later part of the Iron Age and are not in any way related to the operation of a copper industry. Nor have traditional identifications of 'King Solomon's Mines' survived scrutiny. Rothenberg's researches in the Timna mining area, on the west of the Wadi Arabah, have revealed exploitation of the local copper mines by Egypt from the Late Bronze Age well into the twelfth century. By the tenth century activity appears to have ceased until Roman times, though there were active copper mines in the Wadi Feinan of modern Jordan.

What then of the fleet Solomon equipped at Ezion-Geber, with the assistance of experienced Phoenician sailors, for trade with Ophir (1 *Kings* 9:26–8)? Present evidence for this activity is largely indirect. The Old Testament simply tells us that Ezion-Geber was 'near Elath on the shores of the Red Sea in the land of Edom'. Rothenberg, following a survey in 1956–7, has identified it with the 'Coral Island' or the 'Isle of the Pharaohs' (*Jezirat Fara'un*), which has the only natural harbour in the Gulf of Elat-Aqabah. It lies just off the coast of Sinai, south of Elat, and may originally

65 Detail of the stone masonry in one of the door jambs of the gate attributed to Solomon's time at Megiddo (cf. 64).

have been the Egyptian port for mining expeditions into Arabia. Over thirty years ago a sherd of pottery was found on the surface of Tel Qasile, in the suburbs of modern Tel Aviv, probably dating to the eighth century BC. It bears an inscription, with the figure 30 written in the Phoenician manner: '(G)old (of) Ophir. (Belonging) to Beth-Horon/30 sh(ekels)'. The exact location of Ophir remains unknown, but it probably lay on the sea route to India rather than (as some have argued), in India itself, perhaps in modern Somalia in Africa. Sheba, whence came the famous queen, was also in the Red Sea region, but it is not certain whether it was in modern South Yemen or further to the north in Saudi Arabia.

Both Ophir and Sheba were intermediaries in a long-distance trade that by the tenth century, with the increasing use of domesticated camels for overland caravans rather than the donkey which had been used previously, was bringing the exotic produce of the Orient through Arabia for shipment up the Red Sea. As later peoples, notably the Nabataeans, were to show, whoever controlled this sea trade and its passage through the Levant into the east Mediterranean tapped enormous sources of wealth.

In the Negev highlands, north of Makhtesh Ramon, extensive surveys by Israeli archaeologists in recent years have revealed numerous small settlements, many either themselves fortified or grouped round fortified buildings that may not be contemporary. Nearly thirty of these settlements have now been excavated, establishing that they were created sometime in the eleventh or early tenth century and were then abandoned relatively soon afterwards. Some might perhaps have been abruptly destroyed through military action, but the greater majority were not. Explanations for their emergence and eclipse have varied, since precise dating is difficult. For some they represent the penetration of the Israelites through lines of fortresses along routes into the Negev either late in the period of the Judges or under the United Monarchy; for others they are settlements of the semi-nomadic peoples of the region, like the Amalekites, prior to the period of Israelite settlement, destroyed in the wars these peoples fought with Saul and David.

The true explanation is perhaps both at once more complex and more related to the nature of this rugged landscape than previous views have allowed. They seem most likely to be the settlements of native desert tribesmen who from the twelfth through into the tenth century BC found that new resources from overland trade and copper production, stimulated by Egyptian patronage, brought less dependence on pastoralism and an opportunity to settle down in permanent farming communities. When these desert peoples lost control of the Arabian trade to Solomon, following Saul's and David's campaigns against them, they reverted once more to full pastoralist ways-of-life. They then abandoned these settlements, which give archaeologists a brief glimpse into the lives of nomadic or semi-nomadic peoples, who all too rarely become archaeologically visible. The rulers of the United Kingdom then established fortified centres to defend their southern borders against intrusions, whence through tough diplomacy they secured control over the lucrative transit trade from Arabia that brought wealth and influence to Solomon.

Ammon, Moab and Edom, according to the Old Testament (2 *Samuel* 8–12), came under Israelite domination at this time. At present this phase is only documented archaeologically by scattered pottery finds in Transjordan. However, some of them reflect cultural links westwards into Phoenicia and Cyprus, complementary to the widely ranging contacts of Solomon's realm. Material remains of his ascendancy may everywhere remain meagre, but at no point does what survives invalidate the record of the Old Testament.

7. The period of the Divided Monarchy of Judah and Israel

In archaeology, as in history, the period from the later tenth century BC to the Assyrian invasions two centuries later is best studied separately in Judah and in Israel. The differences between the two kingdoms have often been emphasised. The southern kingdom of Judah, centred on Jerusalem, had a relatively stable dynastic tradition. Though smaller and geographically less favoured, it was better insulated from foreign threats and was internally more homogeneous. Israel, centred for most of its history on Samaria, was chronically unstable; it had borders to the north and to the east open to powerful, predatory neighbours. She was consequently more open to foreign cultural contacts and continued the links with Phoenicia established by David and Solomon, perhaps encouraged by the large Canaanite population within her borders. With important lines of communication, good land for arable farming and for cattle-breeding, and a number of long-established cities, Israel was destined to be economically the richer and politically the more prominent. She was also to be the first to fall before a foreign invader.

Judah and Israel hold an unusual place in the history of the ancient Near East. Whereas in other countries the course of events in the first millennium BC has been almost entirely reconstructed in modern times from archaeological sources, for Judah and Israel they have survived in the Old Testament narrative. Whatever the role of later editors in moulding the text as we have it, it provides a uniquely detailed account that archaeological sources have done relatively little to amplify.

The evidence of extra-Biblical historical royal inscriptions from the region is meagre and none has recently been discovered. Clay sealings, bearing the names of officials, are all the evidence there is at present for the papyrus rolls that served as administrative documents, and they steadily increase in number. More widely relevant, and again slowly accumulating year by year, are simple administrative lists and accounts, letters and legal documents, written in ink on ostraca. The evidence they yield may be integrated with information provided by stamped jar handles, notably the royal Judaean series (see below), and inscribed seals, to reconstruct administrative activity and government procedures.

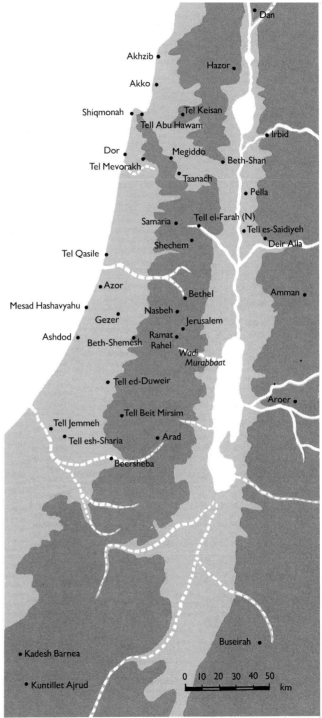

66 Map of Israel and Judah.

Inscriptions that throw light on religious life remain rare and, when they do emerge, are often both fragmentary and enigmatic. Two discoveries in recent years have proved instructive and controversial. They both belong to the eighth century BC: the 'Balaam inscription', found by Franken in 1967 at Deir Alla in the Jordan Valley, and the varied graffiti and inscriptions from the site of Kuntillet Ajrud (Horvat Teiman), deep in the Negev, excavated in 1975–6 by Meshel (76–8).

Readers of the archaeological literature for the mature Iron Age (*c.* 900–586 BC) will be well aware that controversy in no way diminishes when the Biblical narrative offers a more reliably 'historic' text than it does for the time before and during the entry of the Israelites into Canaan. For a period of about twenty years, until his death in 1976, Aharoni engaged Yadin (who died in 1984) in vigorous debate over a number of problems in which archaeological finds of the mature Iron Age are interpreted in the light of information provided by the Old Testament. Their controversies ranged widely, embracing the defences of Megiddo, the location of a possible shrine at Beersheba and the date of that town's destruction, the dating and interpretation of the palace at Ramat Rahel, and the stratigraphy of the final phase of occupation in the fortress at Arad. That two such well-informed and experienced archaeologists should differ so decisively serves to show how the objective criteria needed to resolve such issues remain largely absent. Even in the Iron Age, when Biblical texts and the evidence of dirt archaeology meet, a reasonable element of doubt constantly lends scope for continuing inquiry.

Judah

Concentrated excavation in Jerusalem in the past twenty-five years has focused attention particularly on the city's topography. The primary question is simple: did the city extend beyond the eastern ridge, the city of David and Solomon, across the central valley onto the larger western ridge at the time of the Divided Monarchy? If so, can its boundaries be defined? Traditionally, a maximalist view prevailed, accepting that the line of the 'first wall' described by the Jewish historian Josephus in the first century AD had originated sometime in the Iron Age; such an extension was also believed to suit Biblical references to 'Mishneh: the second quarter'. However, following her excavations between 1961 and 1967 Dame Kathleen Kenyon strongly argued a minimalist case, confining the pre-Exilic city to the eastern ridge, where there was ample evidence of Iron Age occupation. More recent excavations, notably those of Avigad in the Jewish Quarter of the present Old City of Jerusalem, have revealed traces of permanent settlement hereabouts in the mature Iron Age. It was probably at first unwalled, then annexed to the walled city of the eastern ridge by defences built in the eighth century BC. This may, indeed, have been the Biblical 'Mishneh'.

However, only disjointed segments of these fortifications in the shape of wall fragments and gate segments, have so far been uncovered, often at great depth (98). They are still rather enigmatic and it would be unwise to draw far-reaching conclusions from them. They have been widely interpreted as parts of the earliest wall along what was to be the northern line of the later 'first wall' of Josephus, running westwards from the Temple platform towards the present Citadel. They had been reconstructed in Hasmonean times (second to first centuries BC). Where this wall turned south is by no means yet clear. Indeed, the extent of Iron Age quarrying in the present 'Armenian Garden' and in areas northwards, and the absence hereabouts of definite city walls, suggests that before the Exile any defensive wall running southwards along the western limits of the new suburb did so much closer to the Temple than anything described by Josephus. This is not to deny, as scattered rock-cut tombs and Iron Age pottery indicate, that there were expanding unfortified extramural suburbs at this time scattered across the western hill and even northwards to where the present north wall of the Old City runs. But the existence of an Iron Age precursor for the whole wide southern sweep of the 'first wall' of Josephus remains only a hypothesis. Kenyon's negative evidence is certainly not conclusive; but neither is any of the meagre positive evidence cited since.

Kenyon's and Shiloh's excavations on the lower slopes of the eastern ridge have revealed a long stretch of eighth-century defensive city wall that enclosed areas outside Solomon's city. It has recently been shown that a section revealed by Kenyon had a distinctive structure. It was set on a footing of boulders. Its superstructure was of smaller stones laced with timber beams. Along the outer footing of the wall may have run a street two or three metres wide flanked by a thin retaining wall. Together they could have formed a 'covered way' outside the city wall, perhaps for rapid troop movement in times of threat.

Here, as on the western ridge, poor, simple dwellings were being built outside the fortified city by the later eighth century BC. This expansion has been associated with an influx of refugees from the north when Israel fell to the Assyrians. Among these structures was a feature identified as a cult place by Kathleen Kenyon (68); this has been disputed. It is indeed likely that the two upright monoliths, standing in a small room, which she identified as *masseboth*, were merely roof or floor supports. But adjacent to this room was a cave that had served as a repository for pottery vessels. Another larger cave nearby contained hundreds of vessels, terracotta female figurines and model animals, including horses with a disk or rosette set between their

67 The so-called Jebusite ramp on the crest of the eastern ridge of Ophel in Jerusalem after its recent clearance in Shiloh's excavation. His explanation of the sequence is given in the numbered key: 1) retaining walls and stone fill of the stratum 16 citadel (Late Bronze Age); 2) the stepped stone structure of stratum 14 (tenth century BC); 3) fortification in strata 7–6 (Hellenistic to early Roman periods); 4) the seventh-century 'House of Ahiel'; 5) the seventh-century 'Burnt Room'; 6) modern retaining walls.

68 Complex of buildings revealed in Kenyon's excavations (1961–7) on the lower slopes of Ophel in Jerusalem to the north-west of the Spring of Gihon. They are associated with caves filled with discarded pottery of the seventh century BC, perhaps to prevent their profanation after use in cult ceremonies. Recent research has challenged the view, expressed by Kathleen Kenyon, that these were extra-mural shrines for unorthodox cults.

ears. As there was no sign of burials in these caves, they do indeed appear to have been repositories for cult vessels and votive offerings that had to be concealed after use to prevent them from being profaned.

Hezekiah (*c.* 715–687/6 BC) is the only king of Judah who, according to the Old Testament, fortified the walls of Jerusalem and secured a new source of water for use during times of siege, as he prepared to withstand the threat of Assyrian attack in the last decade of the eighth century BC. The most famous testimony to the measures he took is the rock-cut Siloam Tunnel, which probably exploited natural fissure lines and crevices in the rock. It has long been accepted that references in 2 *Chronicles* 32:3–4 and 2 *Kings* 20:20 refer to this tunnel, through which water from the Spring of Gihon still runs. The tunnel passes beneath the ancient city and emerges into the Pool of Siloam in the central valley near the southern tip of the eastern ridge. Since, in her view, this part of the city was undefended by walls at

69 A selection of burnished Iron Age pottery from Kathleen Kenyon's excavations on the lower eastern slopes of Ophel in Jerusalem.

this time, Kathleen Kenyon argued that the original pool had been an underground rock-cut cistern, accessible by a shaft or staircase from within the city and invisible to invaders from outside. This hypothesis has been almost unanimously rejected as special pleading, inconsistent with the Biblical account, which certainly suggests that Hezekiah brought the water source within a set of walls. Exactly how he did this is not clear and the question still may not simply be answered by assuming that the line of Josephus' 'first wall' in this area follows that of Hezekiah's new defensive system. This remains to be proved.

The greatest variety of small finds has been uncovered in houses high on the eastern slopes of Ophel destroyed in the Babylonian sack of 586 BC. In the late eighth or seventh century BC the stepped stone structure at the top of the ridge (67) was overlaid by stone terraces supporting houses, which collapsed dramatically down the slope at the Babylonian assault, perhaps explaining Nehemiah's comments when examining the damaged walls: 'I examined the walls of Jerusalem with their gaps and burnt out gates. I went on to the Fountain Gate and the King's Pool, but found no further path for my mount. So I returned . . .' (*Nehemiah* 2 : 13–15).

In Shiloh's excavations three structures on this slope were distinguished by the major finds in them. The 'House of Ahiel' was named after an ostracon inscribed with names, including this one. The 'House of Bullae'

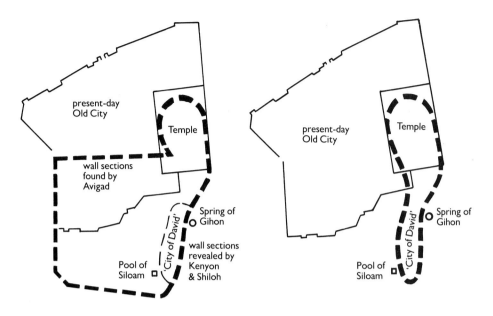

70 Diagrams to illustrate the maximalist and minimalist estimates of the extent of Iron Age Jerusalem.

yielded a collection of clay seal impressions from papyrus rolls, most of them bearing personal names. They constitute the largest single group of Hebrew names yet recovered in any excavation. All seem to be unknown men, save perhaps for 'Gemaryahu, son of Shaphan', who may be the scribe active at the court of Jehoiakim, King of Judah, in 604 BC, mentioned in *Jeremiah* 36:9–11. The 'Burnt Room' produced many pieces of carbonised wood, some of local terebinth (*Pistacia atlantica*), others of imported boxwood (*Buxus*), carved with designs familiar among the ivory inlays of the period from Syria and Phoenicia. They were presumably elements from decorated wooden furniture or possibly ceiling or wall decoration, as in Solomon's Temple. Three pottery sherds of this period from these excavations were incised in South Arabian script after firing, illustrating the presence of people from communities along the spice route with which the Red Sea trade had put Judah into contact.

Just to the south of Jerusalem, at Ramat Rahel, Aharoni excavated from 1959 to 1962 what may have been a fortified palace of the kings of Judah set on a hilltop. It is rectangular, with a casemate wall encompassing a large courtyard and structures whose stone masonry is of unusually fine ashlar blocks. Ten carved 'proto-Aeolic' capitals for wooden columns and a carved stone balustrade, perhaps from a window, illustrate elaborate architecture. The character and date of the first structure on the site has still to be properly

71 Aerial view from the south of the Iron Age palace–fortress complex (the 'royal quarter') under excavation at the end of the 1981 season at Tell ed-Duweir (Lachish) directed by Ussishkin. The palace is on the left. The large courtyard in the centre (unexcavated), perhaps for mustering troops and chariots, is surrounded with store-rooms and other service buildings. The whole complex was separated by walling from the rest of the town.

investigated. The main courtyard pavement of the building uncovered by Aharoni incorporated *lmlk* stamped jar handles (72), so is likely to date very late in the eighth or early in the seventh century BC. It is unlikely to be as late as the time of King Jehoiakim (*c.* 609–598 BC), with whom Aharoni originally associated this building (cf. *Jeremiah* 22:13–19). A drawing on potsherds, found in 1960–1, represents a bearded man, possibly a king, seated on a throne and is so far unique in the repertory of art from Judah.

The best known of the major Judaean royal cities is now Lachish (Tell ed-Duweir), where Ussishkin has renewed excavation on a large scale since 1973. With Olga Tufnell's monumental publication of the earlier Wellcome–Marston Excavations (1932–8) to hand, Ussishkin was able to develop several well-directed lines of investigation. The most important single discovery so far, for the period under discussion here, has been his confirmation that Miss Tufnell was right to attribute the destruction of stratum III to the army of the Assyrians under Sennacherib in 701 BC, not to the Babylonians just over a century later, as many other scholars have argued. Ussishkin has now excavated the great Assyrian siege ramp at the south-west corner of the mound, and those defences in its proximity that it was designed to thwart. This has led to a more detailed interpretation of the siege of this city as depicted on sculptured stone reliefs in Sennacherib's own palace, the 'South-West Palace', at Nineveh in Assyria. These reliefs were excavated by Layard in the middle of the nineteenth century and brought back to England for exhibition in the British Museum. They are a vivid and, in so far as they may now be checked, a remarkable eye-witness portrayal of the Assyrian attack and capture of the city. They accurately indicate the local topography and the major structures of the city as seen from the Assyrian camp (84).

The city of Lachish taken by Sennacherib had been established about two centuries earlier, when the monumental structures of a royal garrison city of great strategic importance had been built to a carefully conceived plan, possibly in or soon after the reign of King Rehoboam (c. 922–915 BC). Not only did the city have a formidable circuit of walls with strongly defended gates, but it also had a revetted glacis just outside the walls, creating an additional obstacle for siege machines and soldiers. The city was dominated by a great palace–fortress, the largest and most massive building of the Iron Age yet found in Palestine (71). The superstructure has entirely gone; but the enormous foundations suggest that the building rose to a considerable height. Associated with it were extensive store-rooms and a large courtyard, perhaps for parades and troop musters including horses and chariots. West of this palace–fortress a massive wall appears to separate this part of the city from the rest as 'a royal quarter'.

The recent excavations at Lachish have also done much to elucidate one of the most fascinating links between archaeology and history in the Iron Age. Ever since excavation began on Iron Age sites in Judah baked clay handles, from large storage jars, have been found bearing seal impressions showing either a winged disk (predominant in northern Judah) or a scarab-beetle (predominant in the Shephelah), the word *lmlk,* '(belonging to) the King', and four place names (72, 73). Three of these, Hebron, Socoh and Ziph are known towns, one, *mmšt,* is unidentified. The two symbols were once thought to be chronologically distinct and lively debate surrounded their possible dating. The new Lachish excavations, during which they were found associated together in the same place in stratum III, have shown them all to belong to Hezekiah's reign at the end of the eighth century BC.

The special type of storage jar to which they were attached was probably made in a single potting centre in the Shephelah and represents an administrative innovation by Hezekiah to prepare for the threat presented by Assyrian invaders to the supply system of his realm. Exactly how this worked, and what precise role the four towns played in the system, remains

Above **72** and **73** Details of the seal stamped on jar handles, from a late eighth-century
BC context at Tell ed-Duweir (Lachish). **72** (*left*) shows a winged sun-disk with an
inscription including the name of a town: Socoh. This type of baked clay storage jar
was part of a supply system devised during King Hezekiah's reign, when Judah was
threatened by an Assyrian invasion that came in 701 BC. **73** (*right*) shows a double-
winged beetle and including in the inscription the town name: Hebron.

debatable. Were they tax collection centres, supply centres or garrison
towns; royal estates supplying royal forts; vineyards; or seats of royal officials
for weights and measures? Most of the sealed jars have been found in the
destruction levels of towns in Judah sacked by Assyria about 701 BC. Spor-
adic examples may have remained in use in the seventh century, especially
in cities like Jerusalem not overwhelmed at this time.

The kings of Judah established a number of citadels along their southern
borders, forming a line of defence against the occupants of the semi-desert
area to the south and against invaders from across the Jordan. The best
known example is Arad, where a strongly defended citadel was established
on part of a site that had been an important city in the fourth and early third
millennia BC (74). The necessity for such strong points is emphasised by the
fact that there were six successive building phases of the citadel from the
later tenth century down to the seventh century BC, each in turn destroyed
by fire.

It is, however, the shrine found within this citadel from its earliest level
that has stimulated most thought and discussion. The sanctuary had not
only been sacked whenever the fort was, but it had also undergone specific

74 View of the Iron Age citadel at Arad (on the hill in the background), taken from the site of the Early Bronze Age walled town closer to the water supply on the lower slopes. This frontier fortress of the kingdom of Judah in the Divided Monarchy had its own cult place.

modifications. After stratum VIII the sacrificial altar in the courtyard went out of use, perhaps following Hezekiah's reforms; after stratum VII even the 'Holy of Holies' had been destroyed, probably at the time of Josiah (*c.* 640–609 BC). The form of the Arad temple recalls a dwelling house with a courtyard surrounded by rooms. The main broad room opens directly on to the court, with a tiny niche opposite the entrance with a *massebah* (sacred stone) and two small altars, and benches round the walls (cf. 1 *Samuel* 9).

Temples are by definition the dwelling of the deity, equipped with furniture and cult objects that symbolise the divine presence. Did temples in the strict sense of the term, 'Houses of Yahweh', exist outside Jerusalem throughout much of the Divided Monarchy or was this some lesser shrine?

75 Aerial view of the Iron Age town at Beersheba in the course of excavation by Aharoni. The modern camp gives some idea of the scale of the town. Its roughly circular shape may be detected, with a road running round inside the encircling defensive wall.

Altars, for sacrifices, were numerous in towns and in the countryside, according to Biblical sources. Among them the Old Testament distinguishes as distinct types, the *bet bamot*, involving a 'house', and the *bamah* (plural *bamoth*), unhappily rendered as 'high place' in English; but it does not make clear why they were so distinguished. The Arad shrine remains a unique find and, for the moment, may be the only real candidate in the archaeological record for a temple rather than a *bamah* or *bet bamot* in Judah outside Jerusalem.

Aharoni's excavations at Beersheba contrast well with Lachish, for here it proved possible to excavate almost the entire one-and-a-half-hectare walled town, which has a roughly circular plan (75). Founded under the United Kingdom it survived with chequered fortunes until sometime in the eighth century BC. A solid wall defended the earlier settlement, a casemate wall the later. Houses lined the wall and a road ran round the edge of the settlement with streets radiating from it as in other contemporary towns excavated long

76 An aerial view of the hilltop building at Kuntillet Ajrud (Horvat Teiman), with the entrance in the foreground after excavation by Meshel.

ago at Tell Beit Mirsim, Beth-Shemesh and Tell en-Nasbeh (Mizpah). Just inside the city gate was a public square and a complex of store-houses; a special water system provided for the settlement. Well-cut stones from a monumental horned altar were found scattered and reused in a later context. Some scholars have seen this as evidence for a temple at Beersheba and unconvincing attempts have been made to locate it. However, the discovery of an altar is no proof of a temple; temples could not exist without altars, but altars could exist without temples and this may merely have been the altar from a *bamah* or similar sanctuary.

In recent years archaeological investigation of the Negev has steadily intensified as a number of important Iron Age fortresses and fortified towns, notably those at Aroer and Kadesh-Barnea, have provided evidence for the interaction of the inhabitants of Judah and the desert nomadic peoples. The most unusual and instructive of these Negev sites is located on an isolated hill at Kuntillet Ajrud (Horvat Teiman), about fifty kilometres south of Kadesh-Barnea, overlooking one of the few wells in the region (76). It was excavated by Meshel in 1975–6. An unusually well-preserved rectangular stone building, with corner towers, built round a central courtyard entered through a broad room with a protected door in one of the short sides, appears to have served both as a shrine and perhaps as a caravanserai from the ninth into the eighth century BC. The entrance room was long and narrow, lined with benches. Two large jars (*pithoi*) recovered from this room were covered with rough sketches and Hebrew blessings in ink. The walls had been plastered and were also covered with ink graffiti. Both this building and a very eroded one to the east of it yielded fragments of painted plaster. Small finds were numerous, including a great deal of pottery and such rare organic objects as a sieve of animal sinew and date palm fibre, and fragments of linen textiles, as well as dried pomegranates.

Scientific analyses of the pottery from Kuntillet Ajrud have confirmed the apparent absence of locally manufactured pottery. The large storage jars were virtually all made in Judah in the vicinity of Jerusalem, though at least one derives from Philistia, from the region of Ashdod. The fine so-called 'Samaria Ware' does indeed seem to have been made in the hill country of the kingdom of Israel, as its traditional archaeological name suggests.

The religious motifs drawn both on the jars and on the plaster derive from varied sources embracing the Syro-Phoenician art of the north and local traditions known from a distinctive type of painted pottery attributed to the Midianites. The site is at a desert cross-roads where a mixture of peoples would be expected, particularly if the incense trade-route passed this way. It is difficult to assess what precise role cult or ritual activities played in the function of this building, which has the characteristics of a wayside shrine. The inscriptions include letters incised on pottery before firing; dedications incised on stone vessels; and texts in red and black ink on plaster. The latter are sadly in a poor state of preservation and have not yet been published in full, but they include religious invocations including the name of Baal, as well as that of Yahweh (78).

Most controversial of all the inscriptions at Kuntillet Ajrud are those including the phrase: 'I bless you by Yahweh ... and by his *asherah*'. It is not absolutely clear whether this is a reference to the Canaanite mother-goddess, Asherah, or to her inanimate cult image. In the Old Testament it is made clear that Asherah can be a deity as well as the symbol of a deity, perhaps a tree or an object made of wood (cf. *Judges* 6:26), sometimes set besides a pillar or stela of stone (*massebah*). It has been assumed that these two objects represented a male and a female deity. Whilst the Old Testament makes it clear that Canaanite deities with consorts were still worshipped under the Divided Monarchy, the suggestion, arising from newly found inscriptions, that Yahweh could have one too is controversial.

The possibility of the worship of the God of Israel and a consort in the

77 Bases of large pottery storage jars as found in the western store-room at the opposite end to the entrance in the main building at Kuntillet Ajrud.

period of the Divided Monarchy was first suggested over sixty years ago, when papyri of the Persian period from a Jewish colony of mercenaries at Elephantine, on the southern frontier of Egypt, indicated worship there of Yahweh and of a goddess (Anath-bethel) as his consort. But since this idea is offensive to some scholars, attempts had been made to explain it away. As more, and earlier, evidence appears the argument in its favour hardens. The Kuntillet Ajrud inscriptions may be read to show the presence of the concept of Yahweh and a consort at an early date.

Some years before the Ajrud inscriptions were excavated another eighth-century text, scratched on a rock pillar in a burial cave near Khirbet el-Qom, ten kilometres south-east of Lachish, had been removed to a museum in Jerusalem. A passage in it is now read: 'May Uriyahu be blessed by Yahweh and by his *asherah*'. Here the same ambiguity has been held to apply: goddess or symbol? Since the Old Testament makes clear how strong the prophetic denunciations of pagan cults were, particularly when assimilated to Yahwism, and how forceful the Deuteronomic reforms in favour of pure Yahwism, it should come as no surprise when archaeology reveals the likelihood of the persistent worship of a Canaanite fertility goddess, more particularly as a consort of Yahweh, in direct succession to her Canaanite partner El. There are other aspects of popular religion in Judah and Israel evident to the archaeologists, notably the wide currency of baked clay female figurines, that tell a similar, if less explicit, story.

As excavation intensifies, new types of shrine continue to emerge. On an elongated hilltop near Horvat Qitmit, south-west of Arad, Beit Arieh has recently excavated a stone-built shrine of the seventh to sixth centuries BC. It has yielded a large group of clay figurines, human and animal, and almost life-size clay statues, including a deity's head with three horns. This device is already known on some bronze statuettes usually attributed to the Phoenicians. Who the worshippers at the Qitmit shrine were has yet to be demonstrated: perhaps one of the tribal peoples on Judah's borders.

In excavations at Ketef Hinnom in Jerusalem in 1979–80, Barkay discovered in a series of rock-cut tombs two amulets in the form of rolled pieces of sheet silver (27.5 mm and 11.5 mm long). When unrolled they were found to be inscribed in ancient Hebrew script of the seventh century BC. Part of the inscriptions on the two plaques has been deciphered as a text almost identical with *Numbers* 6:24–26, the 'Priestly Benediction'. This is now the earliest occurrence of a Biblical text in an extra-Biblical document, significantly predating the earliest of the Dead Sea Scrolls. It is also the oldest extra-Biblical reference to YHWH, the God of Israel.

Before leaving Judah, the increasing importance of surveys seeking to locate ancient sites from pottery concentrations on the surface needs to be noticed. They, and selective excavations, have revealed a much greater

78 Partial view of the drawings and inscriptions on storage jar A found in the entrance room at Kuntillet Ajrud. The inscription has been read to refer to Yahweh and 'his *asherah*'. The two figures to the left represent the popular Egyptian god Bes, always shown with grotesque features (see 96). He was particularly associated with singing and dancing, and was a powerful force against evil. The seated lyre-player, most probably female, has been associated by some commentators with Asherah, or another Canaanite fertility goddess. The significance of the conjunction of text and picture here is controversial. It may simply be fortuitous or they could have a common cultic message.

density of settlement than had previously been supposed in the eighth and seventh centuries BC. Agricultural skills were highly developed to manage water and to exploit as fully as possible restricted soil cover for farming. Security was established through a network of fortresses and towns, not only in Judah but also in the desert periphery, linked by well-defended lines of communication (cf. 2 *Chronicles* 27 : 4) and perhaps using visual signalling systems like the fire signals referred to in Lachish letter No. 4: 'we are watching for the signals of Lachish' (chapter 8).

Israel

One of the characteristics of Israel, as distinct from Judah, in the Divided Monarchy was the rebuilding of the 'Solomonic Royal Cities' and sites of comparable size, such as Dan and Hazor, as major administrative centres with imposing official buildings. Excavations at Megiddo and Samaria in the 1930s had established the character of such centres with their elaborate stone architecture, inspired by Canaanite or Phoenician precursors, their provision of fortified royal quarters, substantial store-houses, granaries and water systems, within elaborately planned defences. They all substantiate the picture of a monarchy exposed to threats not only from outside, but also from within.

The northern kingdom was at first without a capital. Jeroboam I (c. 922–901 BC) fortified Shechem, excavated by an American Expedition from 1956 to 1964, then Penuel (perhaps Tulul ed-Dahab in Jordan) and finally Tirzah, to which he moved the capital of his kingdom. Between 1946 and 1960 de Vaux's excavations at Tell el-Farah (North) (79), on the east side of the mountains of Ephraim in the Wadi Farah, which runs down into the Jordan

79 Aerial view of the French excavations directed by Père de Vaux at Tell el-Farah (North) in the 1950s. They revealed the early Iron Age town abandoned when Omri moved his capital to Samaria.

Valley, convinced most people that this had been the site of Tirzah, as Albright had argued long before. In the earliest town of the Iron Age (stratum III) the Bronze Age city gate had remained in use, slightly modified. Just inside it the recurrent association through the Iron Age strata of a stone water basin and a monolithic stone, rectangular in section, 180 cm in length, convinced de Vaux that this was a cult place with a *massebah*. An enigmatic basin and associated stone monolith at Tel Dan in the square inside the city gate might perhaps be similarly explained. 2 *Kings*, 23:8 refers to a shrine at a city gate and there are Biblical references to the role of water in cults.

Stratum III was destroyed, probably at the time of Omri's conquest of Tirzah. Set into its debris were the foundations of structures more imposing than those found earlier on the site and confined to one particular part of the town. It has been suggested that these unfinished buildings were abandoned when, after having reigned six years in Tirzah, Omri (c. 876–869 BC) moved his capital to the new site of Samaria in the third decade of the ninth century BC (cf. 1 *Kings* 16:23–25). Tirzah appears to have been deserted for some time at this stage. The pottery of the last phase at Tell el-Farah (North) before the break corresponds with the first Iron Age pottery to appear at Samaria, excavated by Crowfoot and Kenyon from 1931 to 1935, whilst that associated with the succeeding early phases at Samaria is missing at Tell el-Farah (North). The fit is perfect. Since its excavation in the 1930s the citadel at Samaria created by Omri and Ahab has been the best Iron Age example of a fortified royal acropolis, with defences and surviving parts of the palace within them built of finely cut and fitted stone masonry in a style appropriate to its status (1, 2).

Yadin's excavations at Hazor between 1955 and 1958 revealed a wealth of information about the city between the time of Solomon and its sack by the Assyrian king Tiglath-Pileser III about 732 BC. The Solomonic city, with its casemate walls (see chapter 6), had only included the western end of the mound which had grown up in the Early Bronze Age, to which the enormous outer city had been added during the Middle Bronze Age. In the first half of the ninth century BC a rebuilding ascribed to King Ahab (c. 869–850 BC) extended the defences some 180 m to the east, to enclose the whole of the original mound. The new wall was solid, and the Solomonic casemate angle at the west end was filled in to convert it into the new type of structure. The defences were further strengthened by the construction of a massive citadel at the west end, where the top of the mound narrowed almost to a point. Another public building had a tripartite plan divided by two rows of stone pillars similar in plan to the Megiddo 'Stables'. The evidence at Hazor, however, indicated that the building was used for storage, with compartments between the pillars containing large jars.

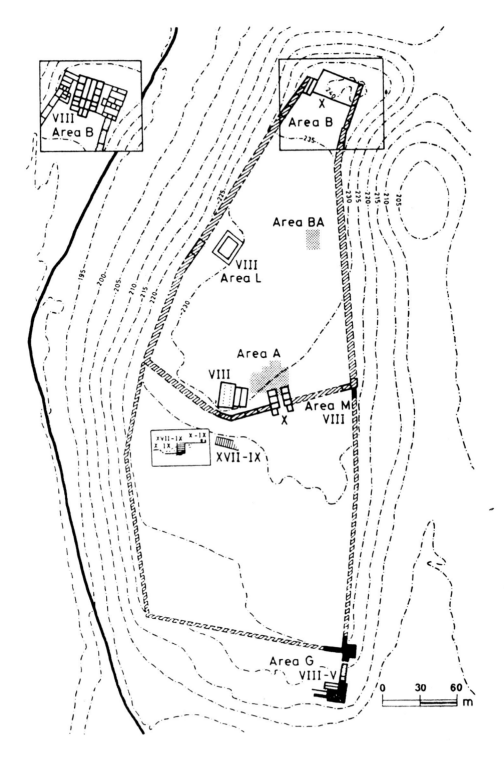

80 Plan of the Upper City at Hazor in the Iron Age (after Yadin), showing the area towards the top cut off by a wall, with a chambered gate, as if to provide a 'royal quarter'. (The Roman numerals denote archaeological levels.)

81 The entrance to the Iron Age water shaft at Hazor, as revealed during Yadin's excavations there in the 1950s.

A further link with ninth-century Megiddo was the discovery of a very similar water shaft (81). This was, as at Megiddo, cut through earlier strata at the top, and below through solid rock. Yadin was fortunately well aware of the necessity of observing the date of the layers through which the shaft cut, and there was excellent evidence that the shaft was later than the Solomonic casemate wall. The total depth of the shaft was about 30 m, whereas the direct shaft at Megiddo was about 25 m to the point at which originally steps descended to a tunnel 63 m long. At Hazor steps sloped down direct to the water pool. The most surprising thing about the Hazor water system, compared to that at Megiddo, is that the engineers concerned realised that they did not have to cut their tunnel outside the walls to tap the visible springs in the adjacent valley, and that they would be able to reach the water level at a point safely within the defences.

The destruction of several occupations at Hazor between the ninth and eighth centuries BC were correlated by the excavator with known historical events, illustrating how a greater degree of precision in linking archaeology and history may be possible when the Biblical sources are complemented by a variety of extra-Biblical written sources recovered by excavations in the lands adjacent to Israel, whence her enemies came. Houses in stratum VI, in the first half of the eighth century BC, yielded material evidence of literate citizens in various inscribed ostraca, and of wide commercial contacts, including carved ivory cosmetic equipment of 'Phoenician' type.

Hazor is only one place where recent excavations have consistently produced evidence to support the view that literacy was widespread under the United Monarchy, especially in its later phases, and not confined, as in Egypt and Mesopotamia, to a closed group of professional scribes. Even so, it is likely that more people could read their own name or a simple message than could write (cf. *Isaiah* 29:11–12). Yet caution remains in order, since it is likely that Hebrew scribes practised their craft primarily on papyrus, now perished. The surviving administrative notes found on potsherds are merely the 'laundry lists' of the day. They may be instructive, but they have to be judged for what they are and not as the normal writing material.

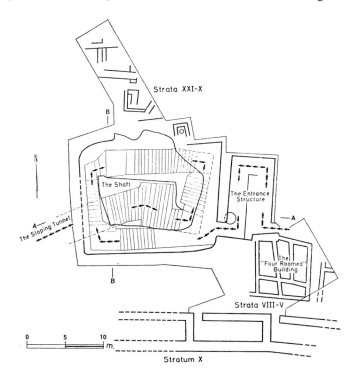

82 Plan (after Yadin) of the water shaft at Hazor, showing its relation to structures in various adjacent strata. The excavator dated the casemate wall of stratum X to *c.* 1000–950 BC. Strata VIII–V cover the period from the early ninth to late eighth centuries BC; strata XXI–X are Bronze Age.

83 General view of the Iron Age sacred area at Tel Dan in the course of excavation under Biran's direction. The 'high-place' is in the background. This photograph shows the difficulty of excavating and interpreting structures repaired and modified time and time again.

The Biblical city of Dan was first located as long ago as 1838 at Tell el-Qadi in what is now northern Israel. Major excavations have been proceeding there since 1966 under the direction of Professor Biran. The main Iron Age finds to date are the 'High Place' and the fortifications. The sacred area at Tel Dan in the Iron Age had a complicated history (83). In its earliest stage the platform, perhaps the work of Jeroboam I's masons, was rectangular, 7 × 18 m, built of large, dressed limestone blocks. Two courses have survived. It had been destroyed in a fire so fierce that the stones were reddened, possibly after Ben-Hadad II's (*c.* 870–842 BC) attack from the north. Beside the platform were large buildings, in part store-rooms, that yielded fragmentary terracotta figurines, incense-burners, cult stands, and ordinary pottery, some in styles particularly associated with Phoenicia and Cyprus. Bones of sheep, goat and gazelle appeared in this assemblage.

In the next phase the platform is almost square, 18 × 19 m, again in well-executed limestone masonry. This time it was associated with a courtyard. A horned altar was discovered nearby and in the area of the courtyard were specially prepared ashlar stone surfaces, one bearing the imprint of two column bases set in plaster. This complex may date to Ahab's reign (*c.* 869–850 BC). In a final major modification, perhaps by Jeroboam II (*c.* 786–746 BC), steps were added to the platform. This sacred area (whether a *bamah* or a *bet bamot* is not clear) appears to have survived the Assyrian invasion and was still respected in the Hellenistic period.

Jeroboam I was the first to extend the limits of Dan beyond the Middle Bronze Age ramparts; but the earliest Iron Age four-roomed main gate, outer gate, city wall and other elements in the defences recently excavated have been attributed to the time of Ahab, following his victory over the Aramaeans, as future defence against threats from the north. Unusually, there seems to have been a paved square in front of the outer gate where large crowds or chariots might be assembled. There is also a unique, small structure with finely carved bases for columns; this has been variously interpreted as a ceremonial canopied stand for the king or some kind of gateway cult place.

The Assyrian conquest and the period of Assyrian rule

Galilee and the northern coastal region were the first areas to fall to the Assyrians in 733–732 BC and their wave of destruction there is as evident on sites excavated in recent years, like Dan, Hazor and Shiqmonah, as it was in pioneering excavations at Beth-Shan and Megiddo. Some sites, including Beth-Shan, were not resettled; but the majority appear to have recovered. By 720 BC Samaria had also fallen to Assyria and this region too suffered considerable urban devastation, as is clear at various sites, among them Samaria itself, Tell el-Farah (North), Bethel and Shechem. They recovered, but only at Samaria were the former defences reused and at Megiddo the new town fortified; elsewhere unwalled settlements covered smaller areas of the mounds than had previously been occupied. The familiar four-roomed house of Israelite Iron Age tradition gave way in the north to the open courtyard house, with rooms gathered round a central court in the Mesopotamian manner.

At Hazor the Assyrian overlords built a new compact fortress on the top of the devastated Israelite citadel, with its rooms arranged along the four sides of a central courtyard. There is now some evidence that at the same time, in the later eighth or earlier seventh century BC, a new town was established in the plain to the north-east of the old mound. Fragments of a monumental stone building erected hereabouts, first excavated by Guy in 1950, have subsequently been convincingly identified by Reich as parts of an Assyrian palace. Its main block was closely modelled on the principal

84 A view from the south-west of the recent excavation of the siege ramp erected at Tell ed-Duweir (Lachish) by the Assyrian army *c.* 701 BC, when they successfully besieged the city.

reception-room suite of major palatial buildings of the period in Syria and Assyria.

Assyrian penetration is increasingly documented by fresh discoveries of what has become known as 'Assyrian Ware', a type of pottery new to the region; some was imported, some copied locally. It is closest in form and fabric to the pottery found in Assyrian palaces. The open bowls, in particular, follow metal shapes and are decorated in ways reminiscent of their metal prototypes. This pottery is found primarily in the north, but with time the taste for it penetrated southwards and east of the Jordan. But even on northern sites it is markedly less common than pottery in the continuing local idiom. Other distinctively Assyrian artefacts, in stone and metal, influenced local goods. The persistent influence of Phoenician crafts is probably responsible for the glass vessels now appearing and for distinctive cosmetic dishes of carved *Tridachna squamosa* shell and alabaster.

In recent years in the Nahal Gerar excavations at Tell esh-Sharia (perhaps Biblical Ziklaq) by Oren (1972–8), and renewed excavations at Tell Jemmeh

85 Crescent-shaped bronze standard and a bell found in the debris of the citadel, in area D, of the seventh century BC at Tell esh-Sharia. The crescent may symbolise the Mesopotamian moon-god Sin, worshipped by troops in the Assyrian garrison holding the town at this time.

86 Pottery jug from a small room adjacent to the east wall of the 'Assyrian Fort' at Tell esh-Sharia. It is inscribed in Hebrew 'belonging to Yoram (?Yeremiah)', seventh or sixth century BC.

by van Beek, following in the footsteps of Petrie, have revealed evidence for the period of Assyrian occupation there in the seventh century BC. Stratum VI at esh-Sharia is the last strongly defended level on the site. Near one fort storage pits sunk deep into the mound produced 'Assyrian Palace Ware' and its local imitations, fragments of East Greek pottery, pillar-shaped female terracotta figurines, ordinary local pottery and Hebrew ostraca. In a more massively built, perhaps Assyrian, citadel was found a socketed, crescent-shaped bronze standard, probably symbolising the Syro-Mesopotamian moon-god Sin (85). Nearby were the chain and prongs of a bronze grappling hook. In a courtyard outside were traces of ironworking installations, perhaps used by army blacksmiths and armourers. Similar installations exist in contemporary forts at Tell Jemmeh and Mesad Hasha-vyahu in the coastal region. These buildings at esh-Sharia were sacked in the late seventh century, but whether by Nebuchadnezzar, by an Egyptian pharaoh, or by Josiah is not yet established. In a number of seasons' work at Tell Jemmeh in the years after 1970 van Beek's team systematically excavated structures erected during the Assyrian occupation of the seventh century, notably a massive mud-brick building in which the vaults of the lowest level were in a remarkable state of preservation. Fragments of large storage jars predominated in these rooms, suggesting basement stores. Fragments of Assyrian Palace Ware and iron spearheads, perhaps from the upper storeys, helped to define the nature of the Assyrian military occupation of this vital staging post on the route into Egypt.

Philistia and South Phoenicia; Gilead, Ammon, Moab and Edom

Before moving into Transjordan, whose archaeology has developed so remarkably in recent years, passing notice should be taken of Judah's and Israel's western neighbours along the coastal plain: Philistia and southern Phoenicia. Excavations in both major and minor towns have revealed the continuing resilience of Philistine culture. Ashdod, whose city gate has already been cited, grew in size, and its material culture, especially the pottery and baked clay figurines, illustrates distinctive local tastes. When the Assyrian king Sargon II captured the town in 714 BC he erected a victory stela, of which the excavators retrieved fragments. North of Ashdod at Mesad Hashavyahu a fortress yielded imported Greek pottery and a now famous ink inscription of the later seventh century BC written on a potsherd. In this Hebrew letter a reaper complains that an official has unjustly confiscated his garment.

Excavations in a whole series of sites in southern Phoenicia, Abu Hawam, Ackzib, Akko, Tel Dor, Tel Keisan, Tel Mevorakh and Shiqmonah, have revealed traces of flourishing towns from the tenth century BC, with typical red burnished pottery and other vessels reflecting close commercial contacts with Cyprus. Among such recently excavated sites is a fortress that may have been among the towns in the 'land of Cabul' ceded by Solomon to Hiram of Tyre and disdained by that monarch (1 *Kings* 9: 13–14). Scattered Phoenician personal names inscribed on seals and ostraca from sites along the coast and inland illustrate how these people, as well as their culture, penetrated deep into Israelite society at all times.

During the past twenty years extensive surveys and an increasing number of excavations in Jordan have transformed knowledge of Judah's and Israel's eastern neighbours in Gilead, Ammon, Moab and Edom. From the ninth into the later eighth century BC northern Transjordan (Gilead) seems to have been a prosperous region with a number of major centres. At Deir Alla in the Jordan Valley the walled town with rectangular houses, of the period of the Divided Monarchy, follows a break in the permanent occupation of the mound and may have been established by settlers fresh to the area.

Initially their pottery was more closely related to that of Syria than to that of Israel and Judah, as are the terracotta figurines associated with it. Only later may links be established with ceramic evidence from sites in northern Israel. In the spring of 1967 Franken's excavation team found, in a room adjoining a shrine, fragments of an inscription written in ink on plaster that had fallen from the walls, or possibly from a stela. It was thought at the time that earthquake action had been responsible.

The work of reassembling the pieces and deciphering the text has proved arduous and debatable. There are two main texts, probably in a south Canaanite dialect (perhaps Ammonite or Moabite) of the second half of the eighth century BC. The first combination of fragments contains a prophecy of Balaam, son of Beor, apparently the man referred to in *Numbers* 22–24 and *Deuteronomy* 23 : 5 ff. In neither context has he any connection with the faith of Israel; but the Deir Alla text is of outstanding importance for students of religion and language. The second combination of pieces appears to be a series of curses, again a literary form familiar from the Old Testament.

Excavations at Tell er-Rumeith, Irbid, Pella (Tabaqat Fahl) and Tell es-

87 Aerial view of excavations by a British expedition under Mrs C-M. Bennett's direction at Buseirah in Jordan in 1974, looking south-east. The planning of complex stone courtyard buildings uncovered on the acropolis here may have been influenced from Assyria in the seventh century BC.

Saidiyeh illustrate town life at this time, but have not yet yielded any finds as remarkable as those at Deir Alla. Their relative prosperity was shattered by the Assyrian invasions that had destroyed Israel between about 735 and 720 BC. Then for some centuries northern Transjordan was sparsely occupied.

To the south, however, Ammon seems to have prospered, particularly as a vassal state of succeeding imperial powers from the east: Assyria, Babylonia and Persia, perhaps as a result of the eclipse first of Israel and then of Judah a century later. In the last decade or so intensive research has revealed increasing evidence of Ammonite achievement in pottery, in inscriptions, in sculpture and in the small finds furnishing tombs, not only in and around modern Amman, but westward towards the Jordan, to north and to south, pressing on Moab. For years the Ammonite language was only known from extremely brief inscriptions, commonly personal names, on seals and isolated statues. Among a slowly increasing corpus of longer inscriptions the most remarkable is that on a small bronze juglet discovered at Tell Siran in Amman in 1972. The inscription tells of the works of 'Amminadab, King of the Ammonites, the son of Hisselel, king of the Ammonites, the son of Amminadab, king of the Ammonites'. It probably dates to the later seventh century, to the time of the grandson of the King Amminadab of the Ammonites referred to in the year 667 BC by the Assyrian king Ashurbanipal. The Ammonite script is closely related to Aramaic, the language and script used in states to the north of Jordan in central and southern Syria.

Moab remains in the archaeological shadows, though now increasingly the subject of new research. The most famous of all extra-Biblical inscriptions from Palestine and Jordan remains the ninth-century stela of Mesha, King of Moab, from Dhiban, known since 1868 (cf. 2 *Kings* 1:1, 3,4 ff., 24 ff.). In 1958 a fragment of a monumental inscription of the same king was found at Kerak, revealing the name of Mesha's father as Chemoshyat, incorporating the Moabite national deity's name (Chemosh). With the increasing recognition of Moabite names on inscribed seals, they, like the Ammonites, are slowly emerging as one of the distinguishably literate peoples of the region. The Moabites, like the Edomites for whom fewer inscriptions are yet recorded, learned their script from the Hebrews, probably when politically subservient to Judah and Israel.

Edom is at present best known after about 720 BC, through Mrs Bennett's work from the 1960s at Buseirah (87), and at Tawilan and Umm el-Biyarah close to Petra, and from Glueck's excavation at Tell el-Kheleifeh, just north of Akabah, in the 1930s. The settlement at Umm el-Biyarah was a simple community of local character. Although Tawilan was larger and the excavated houses more substantial, too little has yet been published of the site for its character to be clear.

88 A selection of painted and burnished pottery from the later Iron Age buildings at Buseirah in ancient Edom.

At Buseirah simple urban development of the type uncovered at Tawilan was found on the lower terraces surrounding the acropolis or citadel, where massive foundations had clearly supported substantial structures. Sadly, the plans were difficult to unravel in detail, but their arrangement of rectangular rooms round open courtyards has much in common with the palatial architecture of Assyria, whose influence was felt in this region in the seventh century. It may be traced in pottery and certain luxury goods as well as in building plans. The threat that Edomites at times presented to their western neighbours is illustrated by a message written on a potsherd found at Arad, probably dating to the earlier seventh century BC, in which the commander of the fort is ordered to gather men from several places and send them to Ramath-negeb in anticipation of an Edomite attack.

It now seems likely that the fashion for painted pottery in Edom emerged only at the end of the seventh century BC with the eclipse of Assyrian political authority in the region. However, it is possible that caution should be exercised in calling such pottery 'Edomite' when it first appears. It might then have been the work of potters associated more widely with the tribes of northern Arabia, those who in the earlier Iron Age had manufactured the pottery decorated with painted designs known today as 'Midianite'.

8. From the Exile to Herod the Great

Until recently the period when Palestine and Jordan formed part of the Achaemenid Persian Empire (*c.* 550–330 BC) has been regarded, archaeologically, as one of the most obscure in the lands of the Bible. On many of the major sites excavated earlier this century stratigraphic sequences for this period were very rare. Many mounds were abandoned at this time and never resettled, so the upper levels are now much eroded. Even where the Persian period is represented the levels of debris are often thin and badly cut about by subsequent Hellenistic and Roman foundation trenches and rubbish pits.

Within the last thirty years excavations at sites like Tel Dor, Ein Gedi, Tel Megadim, Tel Mevorakh and Shiqmonah have began to transform the situation. They offer a geographical spread of evidence which may be supplemented from sites like Hazor where, for instance, only the later Persian period is represented, or caves like that in the Wadi Daliyah near Samaria, where refugees had gone in the mid-fourth century BC carrying vital legal documents written on papyri in Aramaic (see below). Equally important has been the growing number of surface surveys. Here a better knowledge of the pottery of the Persian period gained through excavations has been used to map more accurately the pattern of settlement at this time.

Professor Stern, whose summary of the material culture of this period remains unique for any period in Palestinian archaeology (see bibliography), has defined two major zones west of the Jordan in the Persian period. To the east, in the hilly area of Judaea, to a lesser extent in Samaria, and in regions eastwards into Jordan much of the traditional Iron Age culture ('Iron Age III') endured, markedly influenced from Assyria and Babylonia, who had recently ruled the area, and from Egypt. In Galilee and along the coast, as might be anticipated, established contacts with Phoenicia to the north, overseas with Cyprus and the Greek world to the west had increasingly powerful effects on material culture so that, to some degree, the region was Hellenised before the time of Alexander the Great. However, during the Persian period the most influential cultural tradition hereabouts was

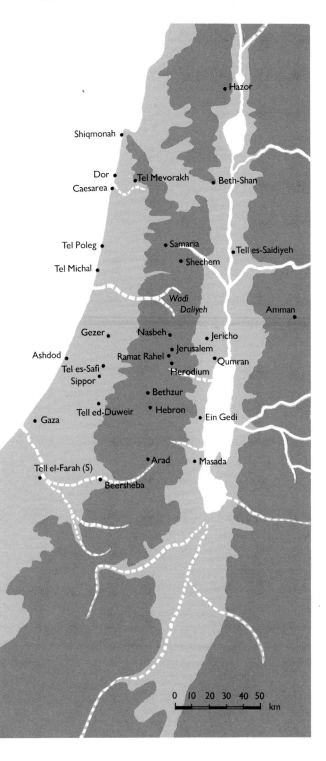

89 Map of Israel and Judah
in the Second Temple
Period: Achaemenid
Persian and Hellenistic
times.

Phoenician; Greek mercenaries and merchants had only a secondary role in local cultural life.

But this is to anticipate. First something must be said about the aftermath of the Babylonian conquest when, for over a generation, Palestine and Jordan fell within the so-called Neo-Babylonian Empire. The course of the Babylonian invasion is well documented. Nebuchadnezzar's army conquered the towns of Judah one after another in 587/6 BC, and laid siege to Jerusalem (2 *Kings* 25:1; *Jeremiah* 52:4), whilst sustaining operations against Lachish and Azekah (*Jeremiah* 34:7), the two fortified cities of Judah still holding out.

At Jerusalem, on the eastern slopes of Ophel, first the excavations of Kathleen Kenyon and more recently those of Yigael Shiloh have revealed the devastation wrought on the City of David by the Babylonian assault in 586 BC. Walls collapsed spectacularly down the slope. Within houses this debris covered pottery and stoneware, fragments of wooden furniture and metalwork. Many weapons were found scattered through the buildings. The pottery is like that at other sites in Judah destroyed at this time, notably Arad, Ein-Gedi, Ramat Rahel, and Lachish. Only some of the towns in Benjamin escaped, principally Mizpah (Tell en-Nasbeh), as it was the centre of Babylonian rule (2 *Kings* 25:23).

At Tell ed-Duweir (Lachish) the evidence of destruction is vivid, both in the earlier excavations of the Wellcome–Marston Expedition (1932–8) and in those now proceeding under Professor Ussishkin's direction. As Miss Tufnell wrote in 1953: 'masonry, consolidated into a chalky white mass streaked with red, had flowed in a liquid stream over the burnt road surface and lower wall, below which were piled charred heaps of burnt timber. In the angle below the north wall of the Bastion and the west revetment, breaches which had been hurriedly repaired with any material available were forced again; indeed, evidence of destruction by fire was not difficult to find anywhere within the circuit of the walls.' It was in this debris between 1934 and 1938, in a burnt guardroom near the city gate, that the Wellcome–Marston Expedition found the twenty-one renowned Lachish Ostraca (90), written in ink on pottery sherds dating about 590–587 BC. Although they were soon recognised as having the greatest importance for the study of the Hebrew language at the time of Jeremiah, discussion continues to this day as to their precise historical significance.

The recent excavations have shown how closely this city gate resembled in plan a miniature fortress, with a central open courtyard and corner towers on the circuit wall. It had probably served the city not just as a gateway, but also as the fortified headquarters of the city's commander. The Lachish Ostraca are commonly considered to be letters sent to the commander of Lachish, named Ya'ush, by someone named Hosha'yahu, located at a small

90 'Lachish Letter', no. 1, is a list of five names, in the form '*x* son of *y*', similar to lists found among the Aramaic papyri of the Jewish garrison at Elephantine in southern Egypt. Some such lists are to do with accounting, whilst others served purposes not apparent out of context. The 'letters' were found at Tell ed-Duweir (Lachish) by the Wellcome–Marston Expedition in the 1930s and date from the time of Nebuchadnezzar II's invasion of Judah, *c.* 587–586 BC.

91 Stone column from the so-called 'Persian residency' at Tell ed-Duweir as now restored on the University Campus at Tel Aviv. In the Persian period a number of tells accommodated forts or residencies for senior officials of the Persian administration. Recent excavations by Ussishkin have confirmed the attribution of this building at Lachish to the Persian period.

military outpost between Lachish and Jerusalem, probably at Kiriath-Jearim. But are they original letters? This was long thought to be the case. Recently, however, Yadin convincingly argued that they were only drafts or copies of a limited number of letters, later written out on papyrus and then sent from Lachish, apparently to Jerusalem. Ya'ush would then be a very high-ranking official to whom Hosha'yahu, apparently the commander of Lachish itself, was subservient. One of the most famous letters refers to signal communications using beacons and, particularly in Yadin's rendering, strongly confirms the identification of Tell ed-Duweir as Lachish.

According to *Jeremiah* (52:28–30) 4,600 Judaeans were deported by the Babylonians, that is about the population of a single major city. So far as is known, the Babylonians did not bring in deportees from elsewhere, as had been the previous Assyrian custom, since the returning exiles did not encounter a foreign population. *Jeremiah* (40:7–12) indicates a degree of resettlement by the remnant indigenous population in the ruined settlements and their adjacent lands. According to *Nehemiah* (11:25–35), some Judaean settlements were able to hold their own in the border areas of the Negev, in the Shephelah and in Benjamin. Archaeology bears this out. Many settlements in northern Judah and Benjamin continued to exist; their prosperity in the later sixth century BC is in marked contrast to sites excavated south of Jerusalem. A viable rural community remained. It is now evident that only the hill country of Judah suffered markedly from the deportations and this picture should not be extended across the country. The coastal area, perhaps also Galilee, unlike the eastern highland regions, was densely populated and does not appear, from its subsequent prosperity, to have suffered much.

Recent research in Transjordan has also refined archaeological knowledge of the sixth and fifth centuries BC there. It may no longer be assumed, as for many years it was, that this region had been largely abandoned at this time. As the Biblical evidence implies, Ammon and Edom thrived and flourished more than did Judah, at least in the sixth century BC. Transjordan benefited from the residence of Nabonidus, King of Babylon (555–539 BC), at Teima in Saudi Arabia for ten years, since then the routes through Jordan were vital to the Babylonians for trade and communication. The Jews returning from exile specially noted the peripheral peoples among their successful rivals (*Nehemiah* 2–13). In 1982 Mrs Bennett's excavations at Tawilan yielded the first cuneiform tablet found in Jordan (92) and it proved to be a contract for livestock drawn up in Harran in Turkey in the reign of the Persian king Darius I (521–486 BC). The same site has also yielded a hoard of contemporary gold jewellery, bearing some witness to the prosperity of communities in Jordan.

In the Persian period Palestine belonged for administrative purposes,

92 Clay tablet inscribed in the Akkadian language, written in the cuneiform script, involving the sale of livestock. It was found in 1982 – the first tablet to be excavated in Jordan – in the northern building complex at Tawilan in Edom. It was drawn up in the city of Harran, in south-east Turkey, in the month of March in the accession year of one of the three Persian kings called Darius, probably the first one who reigned *c.* 521–486 BC.

with Syria, to the vast satrapy called 'beyond the River' (i.e. Euphrates). This was divided into provinces. In the Old Testament it is implied that within this administrative network Judah, favoured by the Persian rulers, was surrounded by a hostile ring of ancient Philistia, Samaria, Ammon and Arabia. Archaeologically the whole area has been very unevenly studied, though surface surveys, particularly, are increasing knowledge of settlement patterns. The coastal region is the best known, from combined survey and excavation.

Many sites of this period now identified between Dor (Tell el-Burj) and Jaffa along the coastal plain are the outcome of a great southwards expansion of the Phoenicians. Settlements were situated near the mouths of rivers and wadis, which were utilised for anchorage. Small finds in excavations, as in Professor Stern's work at Tel Mevorakh near Dor and at Dor itself, indicate widely ranging trade contacts. Within the towns, to judge by documented examples, separate merchant communities including Greeks and other foreigners, as well as Phoenicians, may have fallen under the control of separate Phoenician cities like Tyre and Sidon. Indeed, all the resettlement of this region may have been a case of government planning. In these coastal settlements the material culture of the previous Iron Age, its architecture and small finds, is in a continuing tradition not noticeably modified by the advent of new imperial overlords from the east.

One of the most frequent and distinctive features of the Persian period is the occurrence of large grain storage pits or silos on mounds otherwise largely uninhabited. When, long ago, Petrie first recognised these in the Gaza area he believed that they were supply depots for the Persian army controlling Egypt; but their recurrence across the region now requires a more general explanation. They may indicate a marked trend away from

93 View of the recent excavations at Tel Dor directed by Stern. They have revealed substantial remains of Hellenistic and Persian period occupation on one of the most important coastal settlements of the time.

establishing towns on traditional sites to life on rural estates and in farming communities, for which the silos would have been central storage and distribution facilities. Well-drained ancient mounds are ideal for this purpose when either uninhabited or only partially occupied.

Archaeologically the new Iranian overlords are elusive. Their presence may be traced sporadically through architecture and certain distinctive artefacts. As rulers they seem to have lived in enclaves or military strong-points – 'little Persias' – widely scattered, but linked by a highly efficient communications system. In most cases the sites chosen for centres of control already had a long history of occupation, since they were commonly either at nodal points in natural systems of communication or crucial to the strategic control of particular regions. A typical 'Persian residency' was found on the summit of the tell at Lachish by the Wellcome–Marston Expedition in the 1930s; its dating to this period, and not earlier, has been endorsed by the work of Professor Ussishkin's current expedition there (91). At Hazor as at other places, like Ophel in Jerusalem, an earlier citadel was restored for use in the Persian period. Other isolated forts or substantial administrative buildings of this period are now known at Tel Poleg and at Shiqmonah on the coastal plain, at Ramat Rahel, south of Jerusalem, at Ein

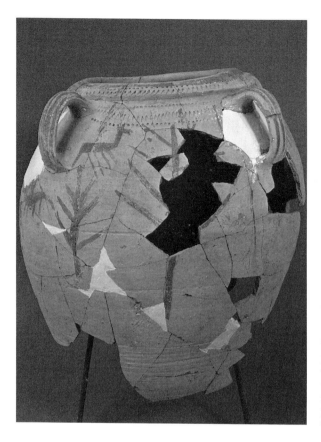

94 An unusual painted pottery jar (restored), of the Persian period, from Qadum in the Samaria region. It shows a camel, vital to long-distance overland travel at this time, and a man riding a horse. Such horse-riders were often rendered as terracotta models at this time and may reflect the Persians' own great love of horses and horsemanship.

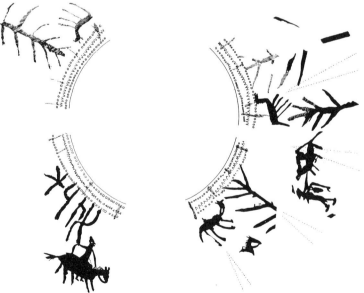

Gedi near the Dead Sea and at Tell es-Saidiyeh in the Jordan Valley, where, at Tell Mazar, a richly equipped cemetery of the period has also been excavated. At Tell el-Hesi a massive three-phase fortification system on the acropolis is one of the largest mud-brick structures of the Persian period yet excavated in Palestine. Such military strong-points, if in no sense distinctively Persian, do at least indicate the presence of a controlling external authority.

The impact of Persian fashions in pottery and metalwork is best illustrated by the contents of a few well-equipped graves, not all found in controlled excavations. Parts of a throne with bronze fittings reported from near Samaria recall the metal fittings from a chair found decades ago by Petrie in a grave at Tell el-Farah (South) attributed to a Persian administrator. Other bronze vessels have come from chance finds in Lower Galilee, from near Shechem, and from tombs near Amman; but there is nothing in recent years to match the silver plate found in graves at Gezer by Macalister before the First World War.

One chance find outside Palestine is particularly relevant to Biblical studies. In 1947 or thereabouts, supposedly at Tell el-Maskhuta near Ismailia in the Egyptian Delta, a hoard of silver vessels and coins was discovered in what seems likely to have been a temple treasury. Four of the bowls were inscribed in Aramaic for the goddess Han-'Ilat. In one case the name of the donor was given as: 'Qaynu son of Gašmu lord of Qedar'. This has been accepted as a reference to the son of the man who figures prominently in the Old Testament as an enemy of Nehemiah (2:19; 6:1–2, 6): 'When Sanballat the Horonite and Tobiah the Ammonite slave and Geshem, the Arab came to know this, they ridiculed us and came ...' The Greek historian Herodotus relates that the Arabs rendered considerable service to the Persian king Cambyses during his invasion of Egypt in the 520s BC. The location of these Arabs suggests they were Qederites like Geshem. This would explain the favour extended to them by the early Persian kings.

In material culture the Persian impact was not great. Such typically Persian objects as animal-headed metal drinking vessels were imitated in baked clay or stone. Occasionally pieces of jewellery with animal decoration recall typically Persian styles. In Judah a type of stamp seal was developed, deriving directly from Persian models, in the style favoured by royal administrators all over the empire.

Archaeology does not yet reveal much of religious practice at this time. At Jerusalem Miss Kenyon took a straight joint in the masonry of the flanking wall of the Temple platform on the east as marking the southern limit of the Solomonic enclosure (95). Thus, in her opinion, the heavier bossed masonry to the north was part of the reconstruction of the Temple after the return from exile, comparable in its manner of cutting to stonework

95 Straight joint in the stone masonry on the east side of the great Temple platform in Jerusalem. The masonry to the right (the earlier) may be that erected in the Persian period on foundations established by Solomon; to the left is masonry in the style favoured by Herod the Great's masons when they substantially enlarged the size of the platform in the years before the birth of Christ.

of the Persian period at Byblos and Sidon in the Lebanon. However, Professor Mazar has dated it later, to the Hasmonean period.

At Tell ed-Duweir (Lachish) there is a religious building attributed to this period that seems different from more standard contemporary shrines of Phoenician type excavated at Tel Michal (Makmish), with some of its cult fittings in place, and at Jaffa. The temple at Lachish has become known as the 'Solar Shrine'. First uncovered in the 1930s, it was reinvestigated in 1966 and 1968 by Professor Aharoni. It survived in use into the Hasmonean period and some scholars would date its foundation too after the Persian period; but this is debatable. The only cult object clearly associated with the 'Solar Shrine' was a limestone stand; on two of its sides are traces in relief of a large hand and a bearded man standing with upraised arms, a posture of prayer. But neither this nor other possibly related small limestone 'altars' endorse Aharoni's view that this was an Israelite Yahwistic shrine, though it was on the site of a very old established cult place. It remains, in many ways, an enigma.

Numerous baked clay and stone figurines have been found as assemblages in pits, which are generally identified as refuse pits for votives discarded by nearby sanctuaries not always archaeologically located. Such deposits are known from Beersheba, Beth-Shan, Tel 'Erani, Tel es-Safi, Tel Michal and Tel Sippor. Scattered examples are more common. Solid handmade terracotta horses and riders are typically Persian; but pillar-shaped figures of gods and goddesses are more traditional. Hollow-cast, mould-made figurines showing new fashions in costume are broadly classified as 'Phoenician'; but more western influences are evident in fresh themes for clay statuettes like satyrs, pigmies and temple-boys.

The main archaeological finds relevant to any study of administrative procedures and fiscal organisation are short inscriptions on seals, seal impressions and coins, and longer texts on papyri or ostraca. At this time there were two main seal types. The official ones bear the name of the province Judah (Yehud), whilst some also have the names of officials, with or without their titles. Small silver coins, struck at Jerusalem by the autonomous authorities of Yehud, bearing the name of the district or governor written in the early Hebrew script, appear in the fourth century BC. They show either a falcon with wings spread or an owl.

In recent years the number of ostraca inscribed in ink in Aramaic, the

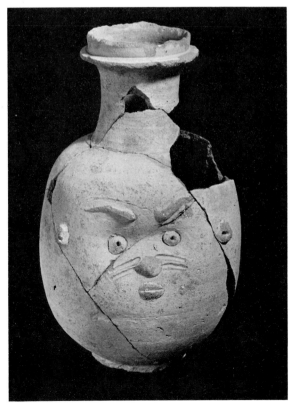

96 Pottery jar from levels of the Persian period at Tell el-Hesi excavated there by the American Expedition in 1981. These are the features of the popular Egyptian god Bes (cf. 78). Such jars, about 20 cm high, may have been used by a garrison of soldiers established at this site to defend the border of the Persian Empire against Egypt after one of its defections from Persian rule.

97 Bronze incense-burner, about 32 cm high, found recently in a tomb of the Persian period at Amman in Jordan. Female figures like this, cast hollow in bronze, were also popular at this time as pots for containing eye-paint (kohl).

official language of the Persian Empire, has greatly increased. Those found at Arad are mostly distribution lists of barley for beasts of burden, with the name of the recipient at the head of the list; they may possibly be associated with the postal system so efficiently organised by Persian administrators. The ostraca from Beersheba, which have been dated to the end of the Persian occupation, list quantities of foodstuffs with dates, generally the day, month and year, apparently reckoned according to the reign of a king, perhaps Artaxerxes III (*c.* 359–338 BC). They may be tax receipts for goods delivered to officials at Beersheba.

For papyri there is one key find made in 1962–3 in a cave in Wadi Daliyah, east of Samaria. Here more than two hundred skeletons were found, apparently of refugees from Alexander the Great's attack on Samaria in 331 BC. With them were some forty poorly preserved Aramaic documents and over a hundred clay sealings from papyrus rolls, bearing designs in Greek and Persian styles. A document recording the sale of a vineyard has a fragmentary sealing of the son of the governor of Samaria. All the papyri deal with legal or administrative matters. The personal names involve elements drawn from a wide variety of deities' names, most commonly Iahu (Yahweh); but also Qos (Edomite), Sahar (Arabian), Chemosh (Moabite), Baal (Canaanite/Phoenician) and Nebo (Babylonian).

In the Persian period economic life was based on grazing and agriculture as before, but industry and commerce, particularly on the coastal plain and along trade routes, flourished. New opportunities provided by being part of a huge secure 'common market' with safe communications, a royal currency of established integrity, and wealthy consumers in all parts of the empire, were many. The spectacular development of the sea-ports of Phoenicia and the coast of Palestine bear witness to the growth of luxury trade with the west, in which incense, spices and perfumes particularly were traded for Greek goods. Inland, however, and among the rural groups the Persian period is not at present distinguished in the archaeological record by intensive urban occupation or by rich material remains. That was to be more a feature of the following Hellenistic period.

The profound effect of Hellenic culture on Palestine following the collapse of the Persian Empire in the second half of the fourth century BC is evident even from a cursory examination of architecture and artefacts. Historical records of all kinds are now increasingly plentiful, so archaeological sources are less called upon to provide the basic evidence for political and social developments. Palestine was no longer on the periphery of a great eastern empire; it was trapped between two contending families established in Syria and Egypt. Egypt was ruled by the descendants of Alexander's general Ptolemy; Syria by those of his general Seleucus. Palestine was claimed first by the Ptolemies until 198 BC, then briefly by the

98 Looking east across area W (just south of the Street of the Chain) of Avigad's excavations in the Jewish Quarter of the Old City at Jerusalem showing, at a depth of 12–15 m, a tower of the Hasmonean period about 9 m square on the northern line of the 'first wall' as described by Josephus. It abuts on an earlier Iron Age tower.

Seleucids until 142 BC, when the Jews asserted their independence under the Hasmoneans (1 *Maccabees* 1–15).

To secure their position the Ptolemies garrisoned troops throughout Palestine in major cities, including Jerusalem, and military struggles were recurrent during the third century BC. Through these troops Palestine was progressively Hellenised; material culture, language and manners drew upon the same source of inspiration. Techniques and styles of potting changed radically to conform with the fashions of great Greek potting centres like Athens and Corinth; the fabrics were thinner and fired to higher temperatures; the long-lived Palestinian saucer-lamp was superseded by the nozzle-lamp of the Greek world. Metal utensils and jewellery followed western patterns; coins and gems bore Hellenised devices. Stamped wine jar handles, found in great quantities at sites like Bethzur, Jerusalem and Samaria with large garrisons, testify to the popularity of wine imported from the Aegean, for each handle bears in Greek the name of the potter or magistrate of the year.

A remarkable witness to the character of this period is provided by the

99 Handle from a Rhodian pottery wine jar from Jerusalem stamped in Greek with the name of the potter or magistrate of the year; in this case the name is Damokles, *c.* 220–180 BC.

Hefzibah Inscription, written on a stone column, first published in 1966. It is a copy of a series of letters sent to the Seleucid king about 200 BC. In these letters the local inhabitants list the abuses of the resident troops, towns raided and food requisitioned, and plead both for the removal of soldiers billeted in their homes and the establishment of garrisons well away from towns.

Iraq el-Emir, twenty-nine kilometres west of Amman in Jordan, is one of the most remarkable monuments of this period. It has been intensively studied in recent years. It is the remains of the 'fortress' Tyros, built in the early second century BC by a certain Hyrcanus, a member of the rich Tobiad family (cf. *Nehemiah* 2 : 10). It is described by the Jewish historian Josephus as being constructed 'entirely of white marble up to the very roof, and [it] had beasts of gigantic size carved on it, and he enclosed it with a wide and deep moat'. The most prominent feature of the site still is this structure, the so-called 'Qasr el-Abd' (Fortress of the Servant), variously interpreted as a fortress, a mausoleum, a palace or a temple and now much restored. As it is still unique, its true function is difficult to identify. At present it is most widely regarded as a temple, providing a link between earlier temples at sites like Ras Shamra (Ugarit) and Jerusalem and those that were later to become characteristic of the Roman East. Although the style is Oriental, perhaps owing something to Iran, the sculptured decoration of lions and panthers and the carved architectural details are Hellenistic.

Although the Hasmoneans revolted against the policies of some extreme Jewish Hellenisers, they were not anti-Greek in a specific sense and there is no obvious retreat in the taste for Hellenistic fashions in architecture. A tomb in Greco-Egyptian style with a Greek inscription for a man named Jason, found in 1956 in Jerusalem, shows the ambiguities of cultural development at this time. One room has niches large enough to hold bodies (*kukhim*), an Egyptian custom new to a Jewish setting, and a room serving as a bone repository, for the practice of secondary burial that was to become customary thereafter. The tomb's painted decoration is an interesting blend of gazelles and ships (a warship pursuing a merchant ship, perhaps a private vessel) and the most famous of all Jewish symbols, a series of menorahs or branched candlesticks, in one of their earliest known appearances.

Small finds increasingly illustrate similar contrasts. In a seal of Jonathan the High Priest recently published the Hebrew inscription is combined with the club of the Greek hero Herakles. Coins may bear on the one hand, Greek inscriptions and symbols of Hellenistic origin, and on the other, Hebrew inscriptions and the non-figurative designs required by strict Jewish custom.

Although, as will be seen in the following chapter, Herod the Great obliterated much Hasmonean building, it is clear they had preceded him in many places. Recent excavations in Jerusalem have shown how substantially the city grew at this time, when the 'first wall' round the city, described by Josephus, was built. The Hasmonean rulers' Winter Palace at Jericho is now particularly well known, following a series of excavations since the early 1950s by American and Israeli archaeologists. At least six great fortresses in the desert, at the Alexandrium in the north, at Duq, Threx and Taurus in the Jericho region, at Hyrcania east of Bethlehem, and to the south at Masada, some now excavated, some merely surveyed, are remarkable monuments to Hasmonean energy and to the skill of their builders. Aqueducts brought water into these isolated, combined palace–fortresses that served as administrative centres, recreational retreats, stores, frontier observation posts and even as burial places.

One of the most remarkable Hellenistic towns excavated in Palestine in the last few decades is Tel Anafa, in Upper Galilee, which flourished from the mid-second century BC to about 80 BC and was probably destroyed by Alexander Jannaeus. The fine domestic architecture, with its plastered and painted walls, its gilded stucco decoration and its patterned mosaic floors, is in the new westernised manner. Metalwork and fine moulded glass vessels,

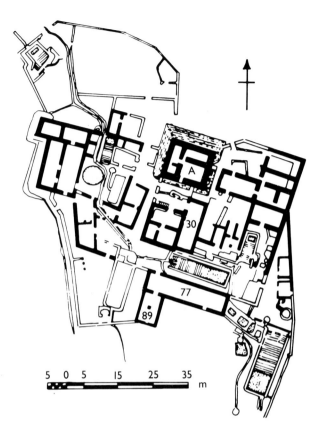

100 Plan of the building complex at Qumran, north-west of the Dead Sea, excavated by Père de Vaux in the 1950s and commonly identified as the Essene centre whence came many of the Dead Sea Scrolls. A is a tower dominating the site; no. 77 was identified as a place for assemblies and communal meals; stacks of pottery were excavated from room 89; 30 is the area of the 'scriptorium'.

many coins, Greek graffiti on pottery and the Rhodian wine jar handles, all reflect the same western sources for fashionable goods and technological innovations.

But perhaps the most famous site of all at this time relates neither to Jewish Hasmoneans nor to Hellenised pagans, but to one of the newer politico-religious groups that are so characteristic of the period. At present the Pharisees and Sadducees are archaeologically unrepresented; not so the Essenes, to whom the famous Dead Sea Scrolls, and the associated building at Qumran, are now almost universally attributed, after some decades of debate. The story of the accidental find in 1947 of the first scrolls in a cave is well known. The cave is one of many in the cliffs at the base of the mountains of Judah, fringing the north-west end of the Dead Sea. Fragments of papyrus and leather manuscripts were found in many of them. On a plateau at the base of the cliffs, slightly above the narrow plain along the shore, are the ruins of a building complex. It has unfortunately become known as a monastery; but it is still unique and the implications of the word 'monastery' are not wholly appropriate. These ruins had been known for a

101 Aerial view of the Qumran buildings illustrated in plan in 100.

long time, but it was the possibility that they had a connection with the scrolls that led to their excavation between 1951 and 1956 by Père Roland de Vaux, whose interpretation of his finds was published in English in 1973. De Vaux believed that his research had proved the case for arguing that this building had housed part at least of the community to which the scrolls had belonged. In recent years this conclusion has been widely accepted.

The site (101) had first been occupied during the eighth century BC. This settlement had been destroyed and abandoned by the time of the Exile. The only important part of the structures of this period to be reused later was a great cistern, into which the winter torrents down the cliffs were channelled. To this many other cisterns were added, since this winter rainfall was the only source of water on the site. Round the nucleus of the old ruins a few new rooms were added about 150 BC by people whose term of residence is thought to have been brief, ending sometime during the reign of John Hyrcanus I (*c.* 134–104 BC).

About 100 BC a greatly enlarged building was established by extending the earlier one to include a two-storey tower, a large assembly hall, a dining room, workshops and extensive water installations. That the meals served in the dining room were on occasion ritual or ceremonial has been suggested

102 View across room 77 (see 100) in the building complex at Qumran. De Vaux identified this as a communal room, used for assemblies and meals.

by the presence of small deposits of animal bones, buried when the flesh had been removed. The bones of animals eaten at these meals apparently could not just be thrown away. There seem to be no obvious living quarters. If the community was resident, it may have lived in the adjacent caves. It is, however, possible that there was only a small resident community which serviced a much wider one that came here only on special occasions. Coins discovered in occupation debris of this phase suggest that it corresponded to the period from John Hyrcanus I (*c.* 134–104 BC) to Antigonus Mattathias (*c.* 40–37 BC) and then just into the time of Herod the Great. According to de Vaux its end was marked by an earthquake, perhaps that recorded by

NORTH
CLOISTER

103 Restored plaster tables and benches, which had collapsed from an upper storey above room 30 at Qumran, as now exhibited in the Rockefeller Museum in Jerusalem. It is these objects, whose original form and function remain debatable, which de Vaux identified as the furnishings of a scriptorium at Qumran, where he thought many of the scrolls were originally written or copied.

Josephus for 31 BC: 'Meanwhile the battle of Actium took place between Caesar and Anthony, in the seventh year of Herod's reign, and there was an earthquake in Judaea, such as had not been seen before.' Thereafter, the excavator believed, the buildings at Qumran had been abandoned for about a generation. This is not certain from the evidence cited and sparse occupation may have persisted through this time.

The full reoccupation has been fixed, from the coin evidence, to the time of Herod Archelaus (4 BC–AD 6) and is always assumed to be the work of the same community as before. This time the buildings lasted until the second year (AD 68–69) of the First Jewish Revolt and they may have been sacked when the future Emperor Vespasian took Jericho, eight miles away, in the summer of AD 68. The site was then occupied by Roman troops, since the revolt persisted in the Judaean desert until Masada fell in AD 74 (see chapter 9).

Early in this phase the tower was surrounded by a supporting wall. Some cisterns were so badly cracked that they went out of use. The debris of some rooms was so thick that it was simply sealed by a new floor at a higher level; a striking instance of this was the pantry, in which the stacked tableware of the earlier period was found. But the use of the rooms generally remained the same, and the remains of ritual meals continued to be buried in the same pits. From the ruins of this last period of occupation the excavators were able to recover a remarkable amount of evidence for the way-of-life of the inhabitants. The emphasis is on the self-sufficiency of the community, with its pottery workshops and its milling establishments.

One of the most suggestive finds was made in room 30 where the remains of what de Vaux took to be fragments of plastered tables and benches had fallen from an upper storey. Near them were two ink wells, one still containing traces of ink. They have been interpreted as the furniture of a room for copying manuscripts. The connection of the scrolls with this building was further strengthened by the discovery in it of a storage jar purpose-made in the pottery workshops of the establishment. It was identical to those in which the scrolls in the caves were stored, usually wrapped in linen. Moreover, Cave IV, the most prolific source of scrolls after the initial find, was in the plateau upon which the Qumran buildings stood.

If de Vaux's historical reconstruction is correct, and it has been widely accepted, it is very likely that the scrolls were concealed in the caves at a time of imminent danger in AD 68, as the Roman army approached Qumran. This has important consequences in relation both to the scrolls and for the identification of the community. All the scrolls, and all the events to which they refer, then date before AD 68. Although earlier works might be present, the majority are likely to date to the major period of occupation at Qumran from about 150 BC to AD 68. People and events associated with the origins of the community are thus most likely to date about the middle of the second century BC; in so far as such things are made explicit in the scrolls this seems to be so. But why do most scholars now identify them as Essenes?

Not only does the Roman writer Pliny locate a village of Essenes at what appears to be the site of Qumran, but information contained in the scrolls themselves coincides in many ways with Greek and Latin reports on the Essenes. Consequently, as Geza Vermes has wittily concluded, if the community was not Essene, 'the only remaining alternative is that the archaeologists have uncovered relics of a hitherto totally unknown Jewish sect almost identical to the Essenes'.

The importance of the Dead Sea Scrolls for modern scholarship is manifold. Before they were found there were no Hebrew literary manuscripts in existence that dated before the Middle Ages. The texts of the Old Testament books in the Dead Sea Scrolls are therefore about a thousand years older than the previously oldest known (AD 1008) Hebrew Biblical manuscripts. At a stroke they transformed knowledge of the original text. Today, with the scrolls from Masada and the Bar Kochba caves from the time of the Second Jewish Revolt, in addition to those of Qumran, the study of Hebrew manuscripts and Judaism in the time of Christ and immediately before is a major branch of research.

In the last century the great French Biblical scholar Renan wrote that 'Christianity is an Essenism that has largely succeeded'. With the improved understanding of the Essene sect derived from those of the Dead Sea Scrolls that concern themselves, not with Biblical literature, but with the institutions and liturgical practices of the Qumran community, this statement seems exaggerated, yet not wholly misconceived. Essenism and Christianity now appear as two independent movements of distinct character in pursuit of somewhat similar ideas, though this does not rule out the possibility that there was a marked degree of Essene influence on the early Church. The two movements may be crudely and concisely contrasted: the one, eclipsed by time, was rigid and exclusive, addressed to the initiated; the other, flourishing still, was flexible and dynamic, directed to all men.

Today, after a generation of contention and doubt, the most trustworthy sources for knowledge of all aspects of Palestinian Judaism in the time of Christ are the scrolls from Qumran. They are widely accepted as the primary background materials for any modern understanding of the teachings of Jesus, though not everyone accepts their exclusive association with the Qumran 'monastery' and its 'scriptorium'. Some might derive from other sources that were broken up and hidden in the caves for safe-keeping at the time of the Roman threat in AD 68–70. If the unique 'Copper Scroll', containing descriptions of treasures and objects hidden throughout the Judaean Desert, is a genuine inventory, as some now argue, and not a work of the imagination, as was previously believed, it would lend support to the view that there was a much wider phenomenon of documentary concealment in the caves of the Judaean Desert as Rome moved in to crush the First Jewish Revolt.

9. New Testament Palestine

In archaeological terms the relatively brief period that embraces the life of Christ and his disciples is often named the Herodian Period after Herod the Great, though he only ruled in the earlier part of it (37–4 BC). However, in that time, as a client king under Rome, he stamped his personality on the public architecture of Palestine in a way no other individual had achieved. He emulated the Roman emperor, not only by building on a truly monumental scale in the Roman style, often using architects and engineers brought from Italy, but also in seeing architectural achievement as a means of self-aggrandisement and as a claim to immortality. There is a pattern and a consistency to much of the work he commissioned that goes beyond the public personality of the ruler, revealing something of the private man whose unusual, and often far from attractive, personality was expressed through what amounted to a mania for building. This would still have been very evident in the major towns whither Christ and his followers occasionally went in the generation after Herod's death.

Much of what Herod did architecturally had precursors in the Hasmonean period (see chapter 8); but his builders dug so deep and built so massively that the earlier structures were often obliterated or left largely unrecognisable before archaeological study of them. Even now, particularly in Jerusalem, study of changing types of stone masonry has not yet firmly identified the many variants in the styles of each builder from Hasmonean times to the sack of Titus in AD 70. But in the past thirty years excavations in Herod's cities, palaces and desert retreats, and surveys of his aqueducts have endorsed the admiring descriptions of the famous Jewish historian Josephus, whose writings are an invaluable source for this period.

Josephus lived from about AD 37 to 100; he was named at birth Joseph ben Matthias, but later Romanised his name when he abandoned the Jewish cause, in the First Revolt, to support Rome. He wrote two major historical works that have survived. His *Antiquities of the Jews* is an important complement to the Bible for the study of Old Testament times. His *Jewish War* deals with the First Jewish Revolt. In view of his own duplicity in this struggle his account has enjoyed an equivocal reputation; the more so, since

104 Stone masonry characteristic of the work of Herod's masons on the western side of the Temple platform at Jerusalem. The human figure indicates the considerable size of the carefully cut and dressed blocks of stone.

he clearly wrote to vindicate himself in Roman eyes, whilst defending the claims of Judaism over paganism. Yet even if it is both apologetic and unreliable at times, it survives as literature. In a good modern translation *The Jewish War*, first written in Aramaic (the language Christ spoke) and then translated into Greek, remains a narrative of unusual interest for archaeologists and of sustained excitement for laymen.

Appropriately it is in Jerusalem that both the scale and scope of Herod's building works may now best be appreciated, though in many ways his most distinctive achievements are in the desert palaces at the Herodium, at Jericho, and at Masada. Only parts of the substructure of the Temple in Jerusalem built by Herod now survive, since its platform is occupied by later Islamic structures, notably the remarkable Dome of the Rock. Archaeology can, however, reveal something of the appearance of the Temple platform as approached from the south, for much of the supporting

105 The south-west corner of the Temple platform before clearance in Mazar's excavations after 1967. The lowest courses here are built of stone masonry in the Herodian style; then successive repairs extend through to recent times.

wall on this side is Herodian and excavations from 1968 to 1977 by Professor Mazar have opened up vistas previously lost.

Herod built here with enormous ashlar blocks of stone, up to a metre or more long, jointed at the corners. Each ashlar was provided with the typical 'Herodian' wide margin and a broad raised, flat central surface (105). They were generally laid in courses about a metre deep and, because of their enormous weight, without mortar. A straight joint existing between the distinctive Herodian masonry on the east side of the platform was first observed by Warren in 1867 and then discounted. Clearance by the Department of Antiquities of Jordan in the mid-1960s revealed it again quite clearly. It is 32.72 m north from the south-east angle of the Temple platform, and from this point south, and then right along the southern face of the platform and far up the western side Herodian masonry may be observed, including the lower levels of the famous Wailing Wall. In some places up to nineteen courses of Herodian masonry have been revealed. At the south-east corner, 'the pinnacle of the Temple', it still survives to a height of about 40 m above the rock upon which the wall was founded. The Herodian platform, which Josephus described as doubling the size of the Temple area, thus added 30 m at the south end and probably nearly 200 m along the west side. Most of these extended walls must have retained a fill of earth and rubble, but along the south side, beneath the Royal Portico, there were subterranean chambers with roofs supported on arches, Herodian in structure at the base. They are today inappropriately known as 'Solomon's Stables'.

In recent years Mazar's extensive excavations have exposed the paved street, originally found by Warren in 1867, running down the slope of the central valley along the west wall of the platform. From the south-west angle he has traced a connecting street climbing up along the south wall to reach the rock surface of the ridge upon which the platform is set. There two gateways, now blocked, may be seen, the Double Gate and the Triple Gate. These lead into passages sloping upwards to the interior courtyard of the Temple. Monumental columns, ornate stucco decorations and domed

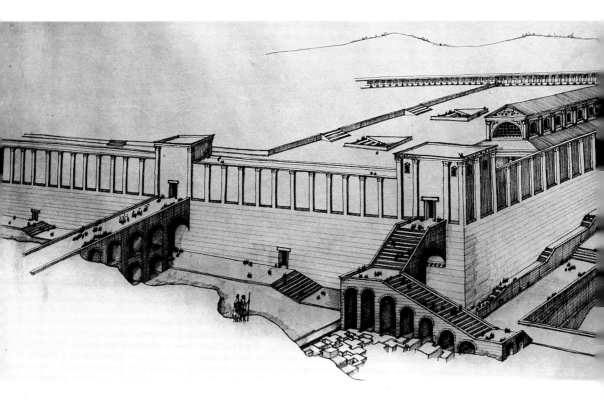

Above **107** Two of the main towers in the Citadel as rebuilt in Ottoman times in Jerusalem close to the Jaffa Gate. On Hasmonean, or earlier, foundations Herod the Great created a renowned fortress spared by Titus when he sacked the City of Jerusalem in AD 70. It has been constantly reconstructed and served a military function through to recent times.

106 After his extensive excavations at the south-west corner and along the south side of the Temple platform, Mazar published this restoration of the southern section of Herod the Great's Temple enclosure with great colonnades and monumental gates.

108 Excavated walls in the Citadel at Jerusalem. Since long before the Second World War successive excavators have sought to unravel the complex architectural history of the Citadel, particularly the date of the earliest Iron Age structures on the site. Still the date and layout of the earliest structures of the time of the Divided Monarchy, remain obscure and controversial.

roofs distinguished these Herodian entrances to the Temple. Outside them monumental stone steps, seventy-five metres wide, lead up from the south. As seen today they are almost entirely reconstruction, but they give an impression of the original layout. In the area between the gates were the remains of ritual baths, where Jewish worshippers purified themselves before entering the sanctuary.

Just north of the south-west angle of the platform there survives the spring of an arch which clearly carried a bridge westward from the Temple. This is known as Robinson's Arch, recalling its discovery by Edward Robinson early in the nineteenth century, and was for long rather romantically visible beneath scrub and cactus bushes. Now it is fully revealed, high in the air. Professor Mazar has shown that the passage from it connected with a staircase leading up from the Tyropoeon Valley to the south. It thus gave access to the monumental Royal Portico running along the whole of the south side of the Temple enclosure, now again well known from reconstruction drawings prepared for Professor Mazar.

Whether or not Robinson's Arch was also connected with a viaduct to the western hill, is unclear; however, connections with the western hill would

109 A view across the 'palatial mansion', towards the Temple platform and the Mount of Olives, in area P of Avigad's excavations in the Jewish Quarter of the Old City of Jerusalem. The houses here belonged to rich citizens and had been destroyed by fire in AD 70, when the Romans sacked the city. This building complex, arranged round a central court, covered over 600 square metres.

have been necessary. Evidence for Herodian structures in the western defences of the city may still be seen in the Citadel, on the right as one comes through the present Jaffa Gate into the Old City, where the base of the north-west Tower, 18 m square and 18 m high, is of Herodian masonry. This tower was probably part of Herod's palace and has been identified as the tower Phasael (named after his elder brother), one of three described by Josephus. This fort was such a fine piece of military engineering that when he sacked the city a century later Titus was sufficiently impressed to leave it standing. The rest of the palace was to the south, where the Kenyon expedition excavated in the 'Armenian Garden'. It covered much of the south-western sector of the present Old City, but little more than fragments of retaining walls have survived, supporting the terrace upon which stood the buildings, gardens, pavilions and canals described by Josephus. Before Herod built here the whole area running north to the citadel, outside the city wall, was used predominantly for quarrying.

Of the Jerusalem that Jesus knew, therefore, we have two fixed points, high points in every sense of the word: the great artificial Temple platform to the east, and a fragment of Herod's palace on the higher hill to the west. In between, the appearance of the city has been much affected by subsequent build-up in the central valley, particularly the main levelling-up for the layout of *Aelia Capitolina* by the Roman Emperor Hadrian in the second century AD.

Excavations carried out by Professor Avigad since 1969 on the western

Above **110** An aerial view of the 'burnt house' found in the first season of Avigad's excavations, from 1969, in the Jewish Quarter of the Old City of Jerusalem. It had been destroyed by fire in AD 70. This destruction preserved a remarkable number of objects including pottery and vessels and furniture of stone. In the lower left-hand corner is a small square ritual bath, to the right is a kitchen.

111 A selection of glass rods and tubes, refuse from a glass factory, found in the filling of a ritual bath in area J of Avigad's excavations in the Old City of Jerusalem. This was make-up for a paved street. This debris includes mould-made and blown glass from the period *c.* 75–37 BC, when the latter appears for the first time.

ridge, beneath the modern Jewish Quarter, destroyed in the fighting in 1948 and now largely rebuilt, have given a vivid picture of the houses of prosperous citizens of Jerusalem in the period of the Gospels (108, 109). Most of these houses belong to the first century AD, forming part of the city destroyed by the Roman general Titus in AD 70 and preserved for archaeologists in the debris of that sack.

One particularly fine house (the 'mansion') of the Herodian period covered about 600 square metres in a series of rooms round a central courtyard. Walls of dressed local stone were plastered and painted with the non-figurative designs required by Jewish custom or ornamented with plaster moulded into panels and imitations of drafted masonry. Coloured mosaics in geometric patterns covered some floors. Down steps from the central courtyard were store-rooms, water cisterns and vaulted Jewish ritual baths, with one entrance for descending and another for emerging after emersion and purification. Vessels and furniture were carved from the soft local limestone; some local pottery vessels were painted in a distinctive style akin to that most familiar on Nabatean pottery; and a mobile stone sundial provided for time-keeping. A fine mould-blown glass jug bore the name of its maker, Ennion, a craftsman active in Sidon in the Lebanon.

Another house of similar type but about one third the size yielded examples of the beautiful red glazed moulded pottery vessels known as Eastern terra sigillata. Large jars with stamped inscriptions in Latin showed, perhaps surprisingly, that the Jewish inhabitants of Jerusalem drank wine imported from Italy. This house was of particular chronological interest to the archaeologists, since it had been obliterated and sealed by a new street layout about seventy years before Titus sacked the city in AD 70.

Debris had been used to provide a proper foundation for the road that ran over the house. One consignment, used to fill a ritual bath, was of outstanding importance, since it contained refuse from a glass factory somewhere in the vicinity. This waste included numerous, varied glass fragments, some distorted by heat, unfinished glass objects, chunks of raw glass and pieces of slag (111). Such evidence is ideal for restoring the procedures of this craft. This find is of particular significance, as it dates to an obscure period in the history of glass-making when blown glass first began to supersede moulded glass.

The precise date of this revolutionary change had long been debated. In Israel the earliest blown glass had previously been found in Herodian contexts towards the end of the first century BC. In 1969 important glass finds excavated at Tel Anafa in Upper Galilee, a site abandoned in about 75 BC (chapter 5), contained no blown glass, only moulded glass vessels. With the appearance of blown glass at Jerusalem, in association with late Hellenistic pottery and about one hundred coins of Alexander Jannaeus,

112 View of Herod the Great's pleasure palace set on the precipitous northern end of the rock plateau at Masada. Far below may be seen the distinctive rectangular outline of one of the camps established by the Romans when they took the rock fortress, after a famous siege, in AD 74.

King of Judah (*c*. 103–76 BC), the first appearance of blown glass may now be more safely dated to the second quarter of the first century BC. But who invented it, and where, remain fascinating open questions: Phoenicia has traditionally been credited with this innovation.

It was in the excavations directed by Professor Yadin at Masada from 1963 to 1965 that one of the most remarkable of Herodian structures was revealed. The incredible fortress–palace of Masada is situated high on a mountain overlooking the south end of the Dead Sea. The drama of the siege of the band of Jewish Zealots holding Masada against the Romans, whose encircling camps and walls are still visible, and the culminating tragedy of the suicide of the defenders in AD 74, is tremendous and vividly recounted by Josephus. There is also a drama in the conversion by Herod of this almost inaccessible mountaintop into the site of palaces, administrative quarters and store-rooms within an impressive circuit of walls.

The western palace, on the top of the rocky plateau, probably the official residence, was renowned for its size, covering some 4,000 square metres. It has residential quarters, in which was a throne room with fine mosaic

113 Some of the Corinthian columns in Herod the Great's pleasure palace at Masada, with grooved and painted plastered surfaces over soft local limestone in imitation of the monolithic stone columns in other palaces where finer stone was more easily accessible.

floors and administrative and service buildings, including a bath house and magazines. The private villa, or northern palace, clinging to the precipitous rock in a series of three superimposed terraces, where it benefited from cool breezes and shade, was exceptional in conception, location and in the views it commanded (112). Nearest to the summit was a block of four rooms round a courtyard; the walls were frescoed with plant and geometric decorations, and black-and-white mosaics covered the floors. On the middle tier was a circular building and other structures with frescos, designed again for relaxation and pleasure. On the lowest tier was a courtyard surrounded by a cloister or colonnaded walkway, with a small bath to one side. Here Herod could not build with the beautiful stonework used in Jerusalem. Instead, walls constructed of soft local stone were covered with plaster and the surface painted in imitation of marble panels, with the drums making up the Corinthian-style columns plastered and grooved to make them look like monoliths. One Corinthian capital, in the lowest tier, was found with the gold paint on its plaster still preserved. Jewish religious buildings at Masada, two ritual baths, a 'religious study house' and a synagogue belong to the Zealot occupation during the First Jewish Revolt (AD 66–74) rather than to the time of Herod.

The Herodium, south-east of Bethlehem, has a distinctive conical shape, rather like a volcano, since a natural hill was substantially modified before

114 The excavated interior of the distinctive round fortified palace set on the artificially created hilltop at the Herodium near Bethlehem built for Herod the Great.

building. It was intended by Herod, according to Josephus, both as a desert retreat and as his burial place. But Josephus does not relate whether the tomb was in the circular building, with private royal accommodation on the summit, or in the 'Greater Herodium' at the foot of the hill. As it has not yet been found, opinions remain divided.

The summit was excavated by Corbo in 1962–7; the lower area has been excavated by Netzer since 1972. The summit is enclosed by a massive circular wall in two concentric lines, with three projecting semi-circular towers and one self-contained circular tower for final refuge. Within the walls is the royal suite on various floors, with a vital set of water cisterns (114). It is a remarkable and total integration of a palace and a fortress, particularly well illustrating the originality that pervades much of Herod's building programme and may well indicate his own close involvement with planning and design.

In the 'Greater Herodium' Netzer has uncovered parts of an enormous architectural complex; as with the hilltop palace, the topography was modified to create this. A large pool, surrounded by a series of service buildings and galleries, may have served the combined functions of pleasure and

115 Aerial view of the foundations of the third Herodian palace at Jericho after recent excavations by Netzer. On the left is a large paved hall and then a court with Ionic columns and an apse. The right-hand complex contains the circular cold bath-room with warm and hot bath-rooms grouped round a court with Corinthian columns.

swimming pool as well as water reservoir for extensive formal gardens. To the south-east is the largest building yet uncovered, set into the hillside. It was probably an enormous palace and had a race course laid out in front of it. An enigmatic building (the 'Monumental Building') with a distinctive character of its own, comparable to pagan temples elsewhere in the Roman Empire, stood at one end of the race course. Its function is controversial. In Herod's other palaces no such temples are known, for he only built them for cities, like Caesarea and Samaria, inhabited by non-Jews. Consequently Netzer has argued that this structure had something to do with Herod's funerary complex; but this remains debatable.

There are many architectural parallels between the 'Greater Herodium' and the winter palace Herod built for himself astride the banks of the Wadi Qelt at Jericho, excavated at various times by Kelso, Baramki and Netzer. This was the focal point in a garden city and royal estate, fed with water through a series of aqueducts. Here again topography was modified to suit grandiose plans in which water, gardens and palatial architecture, in the Roman manner, were combined.

Herod had close connections with Jericho. It had served as a source of supplies in his war with Antigonus, his rival for the throne under Rome. He had used the Hasmonean winter palace there in 35 BC for the murder of his brother-in-law, the high priest Aristobulus who, Josephus tells us, was drowned in a swimming bath on Herod's orders. Here, as so often elsewhere, Herod's work superseded earlier, less ambitious Hasmonean buildings. A fortress at the top of a hill to the south of the palace was rebuilt to offer protection.

Herod's enlarged palace (115), on either side of the Wadi, had four elements, three to the south across the Wadi, one to the north, which formed the residential heart of the building with two peristyle courtyards, a reception hall and a bath complex in the Roman manner. To the south was an elevated building of uncertain purpose with steps leading up to it, perhaps a bath house or pavilion. To its right was a large swimming pool, with an enormous sunken garden to the left running from east to west and flanked at each end by a double colonnade. Its southern wall, decorated with niches in a distinctive Roman style of brickwork known as *opus reticulatum*, corresponded architecturally to a colonnaded area across the Wadi to the west of the palace.

The Herodium, Masada and the Jericho palace are but the best known archaeologically of a whole series of such 'residences' established by Herod. Some were designed to overawe his subjects, and to offer him and his family protection from them; but another Herodium, east of the Dead Sea, and Machaerus in the same area were primarily frontier defences against the Nabataeans (see below).

In his own realm, and he patronised many places outside it, Herod virtually refounded two cities, Caesarea Maritima and Samaria-Sebaste. The latter is best known from excavations by Reisner (1908–10) and Crowfoot with Kenyon (1931–5), which revealed for the first time how Herod created public buildings in the Roman manner, suitable to the status of a city named after the Emperor Augustus (in its Greek form). A massive elevated Temple to Augustus and at least one large stone statue of the Emperor, dominated the city. Aqueducts brought water from afar. As he had even in Jerusalem, Herod adopted the fashionable Roman method for popularising the culture of the day by building a stadium for athletics and also perhaps a theatre. A massive forum and basilica accommodated the administrative and business heart of the city.

A similar pattern is now clear at Caesarea after numerous excavations since 1948. Here Herod remedied his coastline's lack of a good natural harbour. He created an enormous artificial harbour, much of which has been revealed through underwater archaeology, giving life to the vivid description of its scale and splendour offered by Josephus. Enormous blocks

116 A selection of Nabataean pottery from Parr's excavations at Petra, including a painted bowl, a model basket and an inkwell.

of stone were lowered deep into the water to create the harbour, with a breakwater 61 m wide bearing a towered defensive sea-wall. The city, laid out to a regular grid, fronted the harbour. A huge podium overlooking the harbour supported the Temple of Rome and Augustus; statues set up in the city were replicas of masterpieces by the great Greek sculptor of an earlier age, Pheidias. Most of the visible remains of the theatre and hippodrome are post-Herodian; but they are both likely to have been Herodian foundations. Aqueducts brought water to the city; an elaborate system of drainage tunnels ran into the harbour.

With the great increase in evidence for the Hellenistic–Roman architectural setting of the great cities and palaces of Herodian Palestine, and the apparently westernised life-style of the wealthy, it is easy to lose a balanced view of the region in the time of Christ. Certainly in the towns the trappings of life in a great Roman city of the Western Empire were echoed in the public buildings and in imported objects for daily use. A large percentage of surviving inscriptions are in Greek and three types of structure in particular, the amphitheatre, the theatre and the hippodrome, proclaim the impact of social and cultural influences from the west.

Yet, within this context archaeology continues to reveal more and more scattered and unspectacular, but instructive evidence for the less wealthy or for distinctively Jewish elements in cultural and religious life. One striking instance of this, already implied here, is the virtual absence of figural art in houses and palaces as the Jewish tradition required (but so rarely achieved), in marked contrast to its prevalence in cities elsewhere in the Empire.

Among Palestine's neighbours at this time the most powerful and influential were the Nabataeans in the south and east. Originally of Arabian stock, they had established themselves in ancient Edom after the Persian occupation, with a centre at Petra, whence they exercised considerable authority from the first century BC until eclipsed by the Romans in the second century AD. They grew rich on the transit trade in goods from the Orient and Arabia passing west by land to the Mediterranean coast and then by sea to markets in the Western Empire.

Archaeological research in the last few decades in Petra and elsewhere has been intensive, though not yet fully synthesised into a modern study of the Nabataeans. Field surveys have revealed their mastery in creating an agricultural economy by skilful management of scanty water supplies in areas apparently bleak and inhospitable. Research on cities, villages and fortresses in the Negev and in Jordan demonstrate an architectural genius no less distinctive and their fine painted pottery illustrates high technical skill.

Unlike the centuries covered by the historical portions of the Old Testament, the New Testament describes little more than two generations in the first century AD during the early days of the Roman Empire. The world which the Gospels so vividly describe is largely the rural community of Palestine, where Christ grew up and spent most of his brief ministry. Upon this archaeology can throw no direct light, though research steadily increases knowledge of agricultural practice in Roman times. We have to be content for the most part with increasing knowledge of the cities and communities through which Christ passed, and the public figures he encountered. In 1961, for the first time, a Latin inscription was found, reused in the theatre at Caesarea Maritima, bearing the name of Pontius Pilate, procurator of Judea (*c.* AD 26–36).

Stone boxes, in which the bones of the dead were placed after the flesh had decayed, bearing roughly incised names like Simon, Martha, Mary, John, Judas and many others, so familiar to Christ, are among the commoner antiquities of this time. But history conceals whether any of these ossuaries was that of one of the simple people who have found immortality in the pages of the New Testament. This burial custom appeared in the middle of the first century BC and disappeared after the destruction of the Temple in AD 70. It is concentrated in Jerusalem and its neighbourhood as far as

117 A deep sounding cut during Kathleen Kenyon's excavations in the Old City of Jerusalem in the Muristan, to the south of the Church of the Holy Sepulchre. She argued that the sequence of deposits here from the Iron Age, in what she believed to be an extra-mural stone quarry, through to the first–second centuries AD, indicated that the area had been outside the City Walls at the time of Christ's Crucifixion. On this argument the location of Golgotha within the walls of the Church of the Holy Sepulchre could be the authentic site.

Jericho. Whence it came and why it disappeared are still unresolved questions.

In the main very little material evidence of the Gospel story can be expected to have survived. Buildings closely associated with the life of Christ and his ministry have been identified over the centuries. The archaeological evidence more often than not fails to substantiate so early a dating for them, whilst without an appropriate inscription it could, of course, never confirm the association. The site of Calvary and the tomb of Christ are, however, special cases and have long been the focus of a scholarly discussion that has by no means diminished in recent years.

In the nineteenth century, when critical debate began to concentrate on the problem of the site of the Crucifixion and Christ's Tomb, it was natural that many found difficulty in accepting the site of the Church of the Holy Sepulchre as authentic. At that time the Old City was accepted as the only Jerusalem, the City of David and Solomon and all his successors. The Church of the Holy Sepulchre lies at its heart, yet all the Biblical evidence points to Calvary and the Tomb being outside the city walls.

The present site of the Holy Sepulchre is that on which Constantine the Great, Emperor of Rome in AD 326–7, with the assistance of his mother the Empress Helena, began work on the creation of two buildings. One, the Rotunda, was to enclose the rock-cut tomb; the second was a great Basilica church to the east. The site of the Tomb of Christ had been buried under a temple of Aphrodite when the emperor Hadrian created the town of *Aelia Capitolina* from AD 135 on the ruins of the city sacked by Titus. Local Christian tradition alone had preserved knowledge of its location hereabouts. At the Council of Nicaea in AD 325 Bishop Macarius of Jerusalem requested the Emperor Constantine to uncover the Tomb once more. He agreed and ordered the pagan temple on the site to be destroyed and the area of the Tomb to be cleared of debris. In 1974 Père Coüasnon, for many years the scholarly architect most closely associated with recent study and restoration of the Holy Sepulchre, wrote thus about the site: 'authenticity is not impossible, and ... the chances are it might be exact. Nevertheless, in spite of everything, there remains some room for uncertainty.'

As we have noted, when archaeological research began in Jerusalem over a century ago, it was not appreciated that the present impressive circuit of city walls reconstructed in the sixteenth century by the Ottoman ruler Suleiman the Magnificent follows broadly the perimeter of Hadrian's *Aelia Capitolina*, not the earlier city. Consequently, early investigators sought Calvary outside this circuit, failing to appreciate its late date. There are in the rocky slopes to the north of the present Old City a number of rock-cut tombs. Some date from the period of the Jewish monarchy, others from the Hellenistic and Roman periods. Claude Conder, one of the archaeologists

118 The restored medieval façade of the Church of the Holy Sepulchre within which are to be found the traditional sites of Christ's Crucifixion and entombment in the first century AD.

who worked for the Palestine Exploration Fund in its early days, proposed an identification of one of these tombs as the Holy Sepulchre and this, since it was enthusiastically accepted by General Gordon (1833–85), has become known as Gordon's Calvary. One of the reasons claimed for this identification was that the rocky outline of the hill resembled a skull, the Greek for which is *Golgotha*. Such a claim ignores the fact that the present shape is due largely to relatively modern quarrying. This, the so-called Garden Tomb, illustrates the sort of tomb used in Christ's time, and is a pleasant and reverentially tended site, but there is no scientific evidence to support Conder's identification.

In order to understand where the site of the Crucifixion and the Tomb may have been, it is necessary to establish the position of the north wall of Jerusalem in the time of Christ. On this archaeology continues to provide fresh evidence year by year, but vigorous debate continues. The description of the walls of Jerusalem given by Josephus in his *Wars of the Jews* is fundamental to the inquiry. He describes three north walls that had to be stormed by the Roman Army under Titus in AD 70. According to Josephus the outermost, or third, wall was built after Christ's death by Herod Agrippa (AD 40–44) 'to protect the newest parts of the City, hitherto defenceless', so is not relevant to the problem of locating Calvary. This is fortunate, since its exact line remains highly controversial. The question turns on whether it followed approximately the present northern wall, thus now running below the famous Damascus Gate or something like it, at least in the north-east corner of the Old City, or whether it ran about 450 m to the north where, as early as 1838, Robinson located traces of a stone wall that has been much investigated in the last thirty years. This is unlikely to be the third wall of Josephus. There are no returns southwards to the City and no known remains of first-century AD occupation between it and the present Old City, as the description given by Josephus requires. It may have been an outwork of some kind set up early in the First Revolt to hamper the advancing Roman army and its siege machines.

The innermost, or first wall, was aptly called by Josephus 'the Old', since it had been laid out in the Iron Age to protect the expanding city on the western ridge 'thanks to the ravines and the hill above them on which it [i.e. this wall] was built, [it] was almost impregnable; and apart from the

Right **119** Plan after Kathleen Kenyon of Jerusalem, showing the possible lines of the various city walls described by the historian Josephus (AD 37–100). The dark line of the outer walls marks the surviving fortification by Suleiman the Magnificent in the sixteenth century. The dotted lines show three possible lines for the second north wall in relation to the site of the Holy Sepulchre. Since only fragments of all earlier walls have yet been located, often at great depth, all reconstructions remain wholly conjectural.

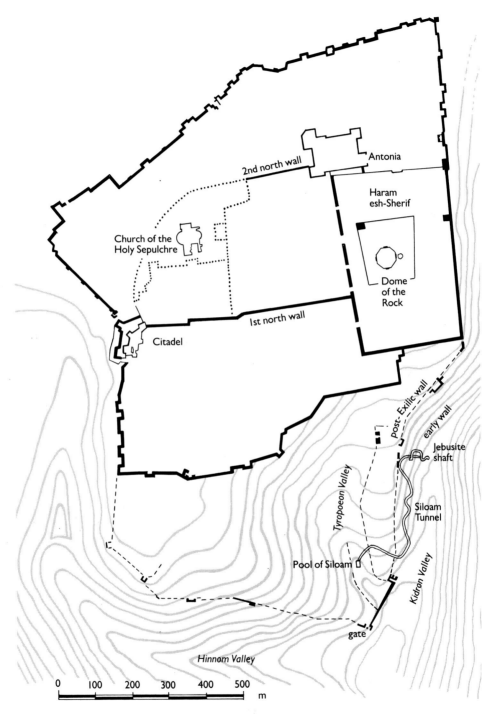

2nd north wall

Antonia

Haram
esh-Sherif

Church of the
Holy Sepulchre

Dome
of the
Rock

1st north wall

Citadel

post- Exilic wall

early wall

Jebusite
shaft

Siloam
Tunnel

Tyropoeon Valley

Pool of Siloam

Kidron Valley

gate

Hinnom Valley

0	100	200	300	400	500

m

advantage of the situation it was also strongly constructed, David and Solomon, and later kings too, having tackled the work with enthusiasm. Starting in the north at the Hippicus Tower [of the Citadel] it stretched to the Gymnasium, then joining the Council-chamber ended at the west colonnade of the Temple.' In other words, it ran roughly due east from the present Jaffa Gate to the Temple platform, well to the south of the site of the Church of the Holy Sepulchre.

It is, however, the line of the second wall that is most relevant to the site of Calvary. 'It started', writes Josephus, 'at the Gennath, a gate in the first wall. It enclosed the northern quarter only and went as far as the Antonia [i.e. the fortress at the north-west corner of the Temple platform].' But where was the Gate Gennath? Avigad has recently suggested that it might be identified with a gate he has located by deep excavation in the heart of the Jewish Quarter of the Old City, about mid-way along the line of what seems to be the 'Old' first wall. If so, the line running north, as Josephus describes it, would be sufficiently far to the east to leave the site of the Church of the Holy Sepulchre well outside the city walls, in an area of quarries, at the time of Christ's Crucifixion. This extends earlier evidence in soundings made by the British excavations in the Muristan in the 1960s and by German excavations at much the same time beneath the Lutheran Church. Archaeology has therefore shown that the site of the Church is potentially authentic, though it has not shown that this is so, nor can it. Here Christian tradition must for ever remain as the primary witness.

Titus triumphant in AD 70, in the words of Josephus, 'now ordered them to raze the whole City and Temple to the ground, leaving the towers that overtopped the others, Phasael, Hippicus and Mariamme, and the stretch of wall enclosing the City on the west – the wall to serve as protection for the garrison that was to be left, the towers to show later generations what a proud and mighty city had been humbled by the gallant sons of Rome'. The British excavations of 1961–7 in the Old City and more recently those of Professor Avigad and other Israeli archaeologists have everywhere uncovered evidence for the intensity of the destruction ordered by Titus. The city was then garrisoned by the Tenth Legion 'Fretensis', who had been part of the conquering army. Roof-tiles bearing the legionary stamp have been found in Avigad's excavations and scattered elsewhere across the city; but still the exact location of their camp is elusive. It is thought to have spread over the area now known as the Armenian Quarter, but no trace of it was found in the British excavations in the 'Armenian Garden' in the south-west corner of the Old City, where Herod the Great's palace had been.

It was, however, the emperor Hadrian, after the suppression of the Second Jewish Revolt by Rome in AD 135, who systematically demolished Jewish

Jerusalem, levelled off the ruins and created a new city, *Colonia Aelia Capitolina*, in honour not only of the god Capitoline Jupiter, but of the Emperor himself, for Aelius was his middle name. Traces of this city remain remarkably scarce in the archaeological record, though its street plan may to some extent survive in that of the present Old City. It appears that the built-up area of *Aelia Capitolina* was restricted to the northern part of the present Old City, where there is a monumental triple city gate now revealed beneath the present Damascus Gate and the long-known remains in the Via Dolorosa of a substantial Hadrianic triumphal arch, popularly called Ecce Homo. In the south of the city Byzantine remains almost invariably lie directly over the layers of destruction debris from AD 70 with no intervening traces of *Aelia Capitolina*. Now Caesarea, not Jerusalem, was the capital of Palestine.

It is possible that it was not until the late third century AD, when the Tenth Legion was transferred, that Jerusalem's walls were again restored to defensive order. It was soon after this that Christian tradition first began to identify those sites that have since become hallowed places of pilgrimage. Here archaeology can give little help, as we have already seen. Archaeological evidence, as this book has recurrently shown, can only throw light on the background to events and on the setting in which leading personalities flourished, not upon them themselves. For that written evidence is necessary and the skills of the historian not of the archaeologist.

Concise glossary

This glossary goes slightly beyond the text here to embrace technical terms increasingly found in books on archaeology relevant to biblical study.

Ashlar masonry: Square-cut stones laid regularly either as a wall in itself or as facing for a rubble wall.

Assemblage: The sum total of objects found in a specific archaeological context, perhaps a building or a stratum (see **stratigraphy**).

Bamah (plural *bamoth*): A Hebrew word used by archaeologists to describe a place of worship in a natural setting outside towns, or the artificial mound or platform within a town thought to simulate it, misleadingly rendered 'high place' in English.

Baulk: An unexcavated strip left standing in an excavation to preserve a sample of the stratification. The face of a baulk is known as a 'section' and drawings of it as 'section drawings'.

Carbon dating: The scientific dating of materials through measurement of the surviving proportion of the radio isotope Carbon 14. At present more commonly cited for prehistoric than for historic periods.

Casemate wall: A wall consisting of two parallel outer faces, divided up inside by cross-walls to form chambers within the thickness of the wall.

Cuneiform script: The wedge-shaped writing system originally developed from about 3000 BC by the Sumerians in southern Iraq to write on clay tablets. It was later adapted for writing a number of other languages, most notably Akkadian, spoken by the earliest Semitic inhabitants of Iraq, and then used as the international diplomatic language until superseded by Aramaic under the Persian Empire. At Ras Shamra (Ugarit) it was specially modified to write the local language in a wedge-shaped alphabet.

Epigraphy: The study of ancient written sources.

Faience: An artificial material consisting basically of powdered quartz covered by a vitreous alkaline glaze varying in colour. It was widely used for the manufacture of beads, amulets and small vessels, especially in Egypt.

Horizon: Designates a broad chronological or cultural phase.

Locus: Primarily used to describe the smallest coherent unit in an excavation (floor, layer, pit, wall, etc.); but loosely used to mean a room or other large architectural unit.

Massebah (plural *masseboth*): A Hebrew word used by archaeologists to describe vertical stones, usually monoliths, thought to have been set up as memorials or objects of worship.

Ostracon: The Greek word for a potsherd; adopted by archaeologists to describe fragments of pottery, bone or stone, used to write on.

Palaeography: The study of the characteristics and development of a script; an aspect of **epigraphy** (q.v.).

Pentateuch: The first five books of the Old Testament: *Genesis*, *Exodus*, *Leviticus*, *Numbers* and *Deuteronomy* taken together.

Stela: An upright slab or pillar of stone carved with inscriptions and/or reliefs. Stelae served a variety of purposes in the ancient world: as funerary monuments, as monuments commemorating royal victories, and as dedications to gods.

Stratigraphy: Is one of the major interpretative principles of field archaeology, borrowed from geology. It depends on the fact that where one deposit of debris overlies another, the upper must have accumulated after the lower, since it could not have been inserted beneath it. In practice, however, there are numerous modifications to this rule, for many acts of nature, from earthquakes to burrowing animals, will disturb any orderly sequence of deposit, as well as interference by man. The various layers of debris are conventionally called 'levels' or 'strata'.

Tell: The Arabic word (with one 'l' in Hebrew) used for the artificial mounds which commonly represent the debris of ancient settlements in the Near East.

Type: A group of objects, or other manmade features, classified together through shared characteristics.

Typology:	The study and classification of **types** (q.v.).
Votives:	Objects offered or dedicated for a specifically religious purpose; often carefully buried later to avoid their use for profane purposes.
Wadi:	Arabic word for a rocky water course or valley, dry except in the rainy season.

Select bibliography

AHARONI, Y. *The Archaeology of the Land of Israel* (London, 1982).

AHARONI, Y. *The Land of the Bible* (2nd revised edition, London, 1979).

AVIGAD, N. *Discovering Jerusalem* (Oxford, 1980).

AVIRAM, J. (ed.) *Biblical Archaeology Today* (Jerusalem, 1985).

BARNETT, R. D. *Illustrations of Old Testament History* (2nd edition, London, 1977).

BARTLETT, J. R. *Jericho* (Cambridge, 1982).

BRIGHT, J. *A History of Israel* (3rd edition, London, 1980).

BROWNING, J. *Petra* (London, 1973).

CURTIS, A. *Ugarit (Ras Shamra)* (Cambridge, 1985).

DALLEY, S. *Mari and Karana: Two Old Babylonian Cities* (London, 1984).

DAVIES, G. I. *Megiddo* (Cambridge, 1986).

DAVIES, P. R. *Qumran* (Cambridge, 1981).

DOTHAN, T. *The Philistines and their Material Culture* (Jerusalem, 1982).

Encyclopaedia of Archaeological Excavations in the Holy Land I–IV (Oxford, 1975–8).

HERRMANN, S. *A History of Israel in Old Testament Times* (London, 1980).

KENYON, K. M. *Archaeology in the Holy Land* (4th edition, London, 1979).

KENYON, K. M. *Digging Up Jericho* (London, 1965).

KENYON, K. M. *Digging up Jerusalem* (London, 1974).

KENYON, K. M. *Royal Cities of the Old Testament* (London, 1971).

LANCE, H. D. *The Old Testament and the Archaeologist* (London, 1983).

MATTHIAE, P. *Ebla: an empire rediscovered* (London, 1977).

MOOREY, P. R. S. *Excavation in Palestine* (Cambridge, 1981).

NEGEV, A. (ed.). *Archaeological Encyclopaedia of the Holy Land* (London, 1972).

Oxford Bible Atlas (ed. H. G. May; revised for 3rd edition by John Day; Oxford, 1984).

PRITCHARD, J. B. *Gibeon, Where the Sun stood Still: The discovery of a Biblical City* (Princeton, 1962).

ROTHENBERG, R. *Timna: Valley of the Biblical Copper Mines* (London, 1972).

SANDARS, N. K. *The Sea Peoples: Warriors of the Ancient Mediterranean* (revised edition, London, 1985).

SETERS, J. VAN *Abraham in History and Tradition* (New Haven, 1975).

SOGGIN, J. A. *A History of Israel: from the beginnings to the Bar Kochba Revolt A. D. 135* (London, 1985).

SOGGIN, J. A. *Introduction to the Old Testament: from its origins to the closing of the Alexandrian canon* (London, 1980).

STERN, E. *Material Culture of the Land of the Bible in the Persian Period 538–332 BC* (Warminster, England, 1982).

THOMPSON, T. L. *The Historicity of the Patriarchal Narratives* (Berlin and New York, 1974).

VERMES, G. *The Dead Sea Scrolls: Qumran in Perspective* (London, 1977).

VOGEL, E. K. *Bibliography of Holy Land Sites* (Cincinnati, USA): part I (1971); part II (1970–81) (1982).

WRIGHT, G. E. *Shechem: the Biography of a Biblical City* (London, 1965).

YADIN, Y. *Hazor: the rediscovery of a great citadel of the Bible* (London, 1975).

YADIN, Y. *Masada: Herod's Fortress and the Zealot's Last Stand* (London, 1966).

Index

Note: material in the captions to illustrations is not indexed. The prefixes Tell and Tel are ignored in the alphabetic sequence.